Babel and Bible

The Ancient Near East: Classic Studies

K. C. Hanson

Series Editor

Albert T. Clay
Light on the Old Testament from Babel

Albert T. Clay
The Origin of Biblical Traditions

Friedrich Delitzsch
Babel and Bible

T. Eric Peet
A Comparative Study of the Literatures of Egypt, Palestine, and Mesopotamia

Leonard W. King
Legends of Babylon and Egypt in Relation to Hebrew Tradition

George Smith
Assyrian Discoveries

George Smith & A. H. Sayce
The Chaldean Account of Genesis

Babel and Bible

Friedrich Delitzsch

New Foreword and Bibliography by
K. C. Hanson

Wipf & Stock
PUBLISHERS
Eugene, Oregon

BABEL AND BIBLE
The Ancient Near East: Classic Studies

ISBN 13: 978-1-59244-708-4

Cataloging-in-Publication data

Delitzsch, Friedrich

Babel and Bible : two lectures delivered before the members of the Deutsche Orientgesellschaft in the presence of the German emperor / Friedrich Delitzsch. Edited with an introduction by C. H. W. John. New foreword and bibliography by K. C. Hanson.

The Ancient Near East: Classic Studies

ISBN 13: 978-1-59244-708-4

Includes bibliographical references, illustrations, and indexes.

p.; ill.; cm.

1. Bible—Antiquities. 2. Bible. O.T.—Antiquities.
3. Babylonia—Antiquities. 4. Assyro-Babylonian literature—Relation to the Old Testament.
I. John, C. H. W. (Claude Hermann Walter), 1857–1920, ed. II. Hanson, K. C. (Kenneth C.). III. Title. IV. Series.

BS1180 .D44 2007

Manufactured in the U.S.A.

Series Foreword

The archaeological discoveries of ancient cities and texts in Mesopotamia, Egypt, and Syria-Palestine began in earnest in the nineteenth century and only accelerated in the twentieth and twenty-first centuries. A few of the most significant early explorations and excavations make the point:

- In 1838, Robinson explored and inaugurated the geographical study of Palestine, especially exploring Jerusalem, including Hezekiah's Tunnel.[1]
- Funded by King Friedrich Wilhelm IV of Prussia, Richard Lepsius discovered several monuments from the Old Kingdom of Egypt during his three-year expedition (1843–1845).[2]

---

1. Edward Robinson and Eli Smith, *Biblical Researches in Palestine and in the Adjacent Regions: A Journal of Travels in the Year 1838,* 3 vols. (Boston: Crocker & Brewster, 1841).

2. C. R. Lepsius, *Denkmäler aus Aegypten und Aethiopien,* 12 vols. (Berlin: Nicolaische Buchhandlung, 1849–56).

- The earliest treasures of Assyria were excavated by Layard at Calah (Nimrud) and Botta at Nineveh (the Kuyunjik mound in Mosul) in the 1840s.[3]
- Sir W. K. Loftus carried out the earliest explorations of Ur (Tell Muqqayyar) in 1849. But it was Wooley who did the systematic excavations almost seventy-five years later (1922–34).[4]
- Charles Warren surveyed the topography of Jerusalem and the temple mount in 1867 and 1870.
- The ancient Egyptian sites of Tanis and Gizeh were explored by Sir Flinders Petrie in the 1880s.[5]

---

3. Austen Henry Layard, *Nineveh and Its Remains,* 2 vols. (New York: Putnam, 1849); idem, *Discoveries in the Ruins of Nineveh and Babylon* (New York: Harper, 1853); Paul Émile Botta, *Monument de Ninive* (Paris: Imprimerie Nationale, 1849–50).

4. C. L. Wooley, *Ur Excavations,* 10 vols. (London: Oxford University Press, 1927–74).

5. W. M. Flinders Petrie, *Tanis,* 2 vols. (Egypt Exploration Fund, 1880–1888); idem, *The Pyramids and Temples of Gizeh* (London: Field & Tuer, 1883).

- The University of Pennsylvania began excavations of Nippur (southeast of Baghdad) in 1889.[6]
- Under the auspices of the Deutsche Orient-Gesellschaft (German Orient Association), Koldewey excavated Babylon (part of modern Baghdad) from 1899 to 1918.[7]

The remains of ancient societies often require decades to unearth, but much longer to interpret and understand. The methods of archaeology have progressed dramatically in recent years. Archaeologists have continuously refined their tools, methods, and techniques. Today archaeology is characterized by pottery identification, classification, and cataloging; disciplined excavation of "squares"; use of sophisticated electronics, such as GPS, infrared, and computer-aided design; and the integration of multiple methodologies, such as epigraphy, art history, physical anthropology, paleobotany, and climatology.

The interpretation of ancient Near Eastern history and cul-tures has also progressed. An increasing number of documents has been unearthed. The vast document

---

6. Clarence S. Fisher, *Excavations at Nippur* (Philadelphia: Babylonian Expedition of the University of Pennsylvania, 1905).

7. Robert Koldewey, *The Excavations at Babylon,* trans. Agnes S. Johns (London: Macmillan, 1914).

collections from Tel el-Amarna, Nippur, Mari, Nuzi, Ebla, Ugarit, and the Dead Sea caves are just some of the more spectacular examples. These provide an enormous amount of detail about the royal administrations, business transactions, land tenure systems, taxes, political propaganda, mythologies, marriage practices, and much more. And things that sometimes seem unique about one culture at first look often fit into larger patterns of relationship when the surrounding cultures are better understood.

The Ancient Near East: Classic Studies (**ANECS**) reprints classic works that have brought the results of archaeology, textual, and historical investigations to audiences of scholars, students, and the general public. While the discussions continue and the results of earlier investigations are continuously re-examined, these classic works remain of interest and importance.

—K. C. Hanson
Series Editor

Bibliography

Beyerlin, Walter, editor. *Near Eastern Religious Texts Relating to the Old Testament.* Translated by John Bowden. Old Testament Library. Philadelphia: Westminster, 1978.

Bienkowski, Piotr, and Alan Millard, editors. *Dictionary of the Ancient Near East.* Philadelphia: University of Pennsylvania Press, 2000.

Bottéro, Jean. *Mesopotamia: Writing, Reasoning, and the Gods.* Translated by Zainab Bahrani. Chicago: University of Chicago Press, 1992.

Clay, Albert T. *Light on the Old Testament from Babel.* 1909. Reprinted, Ancient Texts and Translations. Eugene, OR: Wipf & Stock, 2005.

——. *Babylonian Epics, Hymns, Omens, and Other Texts.* 1923. Reprinted, Ancient Texts and Translations. Eugene, OR: Wipf & Stock, 2005.

Craig, James A. *Assyrian and Babylonian Religious Texts.* 2 vols. Assyriologische Bibliothek 13. Leipzig: Hinrichs, 1895–97.

Dalley, Stephanie. *Myths from Mesopotamia.* Oxford: Oxford University Press, 1989.

Finkelstein, Jacob L. "Bible and Babel: A Comparative Study of the Hebrew and Babylonian Religious Spirit." *Commentary* 26.5 (1958) 431–44

Gordon, Cyrus H., and Gary A. Rendsburg. *The Bible and the Ancient Near East*. 4th ed. New York: Norton, 1997.

Gunkel, Hermann. *Israel and Babylon: The Influence of Babylon on the Religion of Israel (A Reply to Delitzsch)*. Philadelphia: McVey, 1904.

——. *Genesis*. Translated by Mark E. Biddle. Mercer Library of Biblical Studies. Macon, GA: Mercer University Press, 1997.

——. *Creation and Chaos in the Primeval Era and the Eschaton: Religio-Historical Study of Genesis 1 and Revelation 12*. Translated by K. William Whitney Jr. Biblical Resources Series. Grand Rapids: Eerdmans, 2006.

Hallo, William W., and William Kelly Simpson. *The Ancient Near East: A History*. 2d ed. Fort Worth: Harcourt Brace College, 1998.

Hallo, William W., and K. Lawson Younger Jr., editors. *The Context of Scripture. Vol. 1: Canonical Compositions from the Biblical World*. Leiden: Brill, 1997.

Hilprecht, H. V. *The Earliest Version of the Babylonian Deluge Story and the Temple Library of Nippur*. The Babylonian Expedition of the University of Pennsylvania 5/5. Philadelphia: University of Pennsylvania, 1911.

Huffmon, Herbert B. "Babel und Bibel: The Encounter Between Babylon and the Bible." *Michigan Quarterly Review* 22 (1983) 309–20. Reprinted in *Backgrounds for the Bible,* edited by Michael Patrick O'Connor and David Noel Freedman. Winona Lake, Ind.: Eisenbrauns, 1987.

Jeremias, Alfred. *The Old Testament in the Light of the Ancient East.* 2 vols. Translated by C. L. Beaumont. Edited by C. H. W. Johns. Theological Translation Library 28–29. New York: Putnam, 1911.

Johanning, Klaus, *Der Bibel-Babel-Streit: Eine forschungsgeschichtliche Studie.* Europäische Hochschulschriften 343. Frankfurt: Lang, 1988.

King, Leonard W. *The Seven Tablets of Creation.* 2 vols. Lon-don: Luzac, 1902.

Larsen, Mogens Trolle. "The 'Babel/Bible' Controversy and Its Aftermath." In *Civilizations of the Ancient Near East,* edited by Jack M. Sasson, 1:95–106. New York: Scribners, 1995.

Lehmann, Reinhard G. *Friedrich Delitzsch und der Babel-Bibel Streit.* Orbis biblicus et orientalis 133. Göttingen: Vanden-hoeck & Ruprecht, 1994.

Pritchard, James B., editor. *Ancient Near Eastern Texts Relating to the Old Testament.* 3d ed. Princeton: Princeton University Press, 1969.

Rogers, Robert William. *The Religion of Babylonia and Assyria, Especially in Its Relations to Israel.* New York: Eaton & Mains, 1908.

——. *Cuneiform Parallels to the Old Testament.* 2d ed. 1926. Reprinted, Ancient Texts and Translations. Eugene, OR: Wipf & Stock, 2005.

Saggs, H. W. F. *Civilization before Greece and Rome.* New Haven: Yale University Press, 1989.

Sasson, Jack M., editor. *Civilizations of the Ancient Near East.* 4 vols. New York: Scribners, 1995.

Snell, Daniel C. *Life in the Ancient Near East, 3100–332 B.C.E.* New Haven: Yale University Press, 1997.

Thomas, D. Winton, editor. *Documents from Old Testament Times.* London: Nelson, 1958. Reprinted Eugene, OR: Wipf & Stock, 2005.

Toy, Crawford. "Panbabylonianism." *Harvard Theological Review* 3 (1910) 47–84.

Van de Mieroop, Marc. *A History of the Ancient Near East, ca. 3000–323 BC.* Blackwell History of the Ancient World. Malden, Mass.: Blackwell, 2004.

Vries, Jan de. "Panbabylonianism." In *The Study of Religion: A Historical Approach,* 95–98. Translated with an Introduction by Kees W. Bolle. New York: Harcourt Brace & World Inc., 1967.

Introduction

THE announcement that Professor Friedrich Delitzsch, the great Assyriologist, had been granted leave to deliver a lecture upon the relations between the Bible and the recent results of cuneiform research, in the august presence of the Kaiser and the Court, naturally caused a great sensation; in Germany first, and, as a wider circle, wherever men feel interest in the progress of Science. The lecture was duly delivered on the 13th of January 1902, and repeated on the 1st of February.

Some reports of the general tenour of the discourse reached the outside world, and it was evident that matters of the greatest interest were involved. In due course appeared a small book with the text of the lecture, adorned with a number of striking pictures of the ancient monuments. This was the now celebrated *Babel und Bibel.*

The title was a neat one, emphasizing the close relation between the results of cuneiform studies and the more familiar facts of the Bible. The greater part of these relationships was well known, not only to Assyriologists, but also to all interested in Biblical Archæology. Those who had glanced through the recent aids to Bible study, Hastings' *Dictionary of the Bible,* the *Encyclopædia Biblica,* or even the humbler guides compiled for Sunday School teachers, in this country and in America, felt themselves on very familiar ground. The chief cause for pleasure was that it was all so freshly and temperately set out. No doubt some felt a little disappointed at so conservative a treatment. Those who were familiar with recent work, such as is so ably summarized in the third edition of Schrader's *Cuneiform Inscriptions and the Old*

Testament, felt that the Professor had been rather too sparing of his parallels. But, we reflected, there are limits to what one can put in a popular lecture. Many of us knew the cautious, deliberate way in which Professor Delitzsch had always set out his views, and the reluctance he had always shewn to make use of what he had not discovered, or at least worked out, for himself. Hence we were convinced that he had only stated what he felt to be indisputable. It was very readable, and would, we hoped, be widely read and digested as a preparation for further advance.

It came, therefore, as a shock of surprise to find that rejoinders were being issued. A rapid succession of articles, reviews, and replies appeared in newspapers and magazines, and a whole crowd of pamphlets and books. These regarded the lecture from many varied points of view, mostly with disapproval. The champions of the older learnings assailed it from all sides. Even those who had been forward to admit nothing but a human side to the history and literature of Israel were eager to fall on the new pretender to public favour; and, to the astonishment of many, there arose a literature *zum Streit um Bibel und Babel.*

As the echoes of this conflict reached our ears, we seemed to gather that the higher critics, usually known for their destructive habits, were now engaged in defending, in some way, the Bible against the attacks of an archæologist and cuneiform scholar. This seemed a reversal of the order of nature. We had been used to regard the archæologist, especially the Assyriologist, as one who had rescued much of the Bible history from the scepticism of literary critics. Some of the archæological defences had seemed to yield too much, but we felt that more knowledge would improve that. Confidence was not much shaken. Had we not in our own British Museum the greatest collection of material in the world for the elucidation of Scripture, which was being issued as rapidly as the meagre resources devoted to such purposes allow? Had we not scholars amongst us who were fully cognisant of all that could be said on such points? They had sounded no note of alarm. They were evidently firmly convinced of the truth of the old familiar watchwords. Could we be disturbed when the chief efforts of the Church were being directed to the support of a government who would secure to it the ownership of its school buildings? We could hardly dream that indifference to Church teaching was ultimately due to a conviction of its worthlessness.

Some of the attacks on the position taken by Professor Delitzsch were so evidently unfair, and based on such scanty knowledge of at least one side of his argument, that we rather wondered at his silence. The attacks almost answered themselves, yet we wondered at the self-restraint which refrained from scoring an easy victory. Then we learnt the reason. The Professor was in Babylonia itself. When he came back there would be a bad time for some people.

So when the great Professor was once more bidden to deliver a lecture in the presence of the Kaiser and the Court, which took place on the 12th of January 1903, we expected to have some hard hitting. But that was, after all, scarcely the place for a polemic, and we must be grateful for the new and valuable contributions to knowledge which it contained. One could not fairly expect to know the chief results of German exploration in Babylonia, but there is much that is new and helpful.

But now reports of a very disquieting nature reached us. Our papers had it from their correspondents that a very direct attack was made on Holy Scripture, and even, it was not obscurely hinted, on the fundamental doctrines of the Catholic Faith. The storm broke out afresh in Germany, and spread hither also. We learnt, to our amazement, not exactly realizing the Kaiser's position as *Summus Episcopus*, that he had seen fit to address a letter, the text of which appeared in the *Times* of February 25th.

That lectures, even on such an interesting subject, could lead to measures of such high state policy was a guarantee that the matter had passed beyond the circles of scholarship and research, and was become a matter of national concern. We could not afford to remain longer in ignorance of what had stirred our allies so profoundly. We dared not trust to newspapers alone; but, failing Blue Books on the subject, had better read for ourselves what Professor Delitzsch had said. Hence the present translation has been called for.

The reader will not fail to recognize that these are lectures. The opening words of the first lecture evidently join on to some report upon the work done by the German Oriental Society's explorers in the East. Theirs are "these labours." "Babel" is what we ordinarily call Babylon and Babylonia. Many phrases are not such as one would write in a treatise, and evidently are appropriate to a lecture illustrated by diagrams. The reader will meet with many quotations from the Bible in an unfamiliar form. They are the Professor's own translations direct from the Hebrew, or Greek, into German, retranslated into English. Where, however, the usual version would serve as well, it has been given in place of a fresh rendering. Other familiar forms are retained, when no mistake is likely to arise. Thus Yahwè is so well established in English usage that there seemed no reason to use Jahve, except where the likeness to Jahu, etc., was important. The *I* in such words as Iašûb is, of course, the German *J*, our *Y*. So, too, the *v* is sounded like our *w*. The German always writes Sardanapallus for the name of the Assyrian king, son of Esarhaddon, who appears in Ezra iv. 10 as Asnapper, but has been known in England for many years as Ashur-bânipal, a form more closely recalling the original than the Greek does. The mark under *h* in such words as Ḫammurabi denotes that the letter is sounded like *ch* in *loch*, and is often rendered by writing *kh*.

But in early Babylonian times the sound could hardly have been so distinct, for it is often dropped, *e.g.* we find also Ammu-rabi. In the Assyrian or Babylonian words *š* is written for *sh*; *ṣ* for *ts*, or *st*; *ḳ* for a sign often rendered *q*; and *ṭ* represents the Hebrew *teth*, not *tau*.

To Professor Delitzsch belongs the high credit of having discerned the true meaning of those fragments of an earlier legislation preserved, in late copies, in the Library of Ashurbânipal. They had been called a Code Ashurbânipal, and Dr. Meissner had already pointed out their great likeness to the contracts of the First Dynasty of Babylon. But apart from what was said on p. 35, Professor Delitzsch had already, in December 1901, applied the name Code Ḫammurabi to them, practically at the very moment when the fuller text of that Code was being unearthed at Susa. Anyone who cares to read the article in the *Beiträge zur Assyriologie*, iv. pp. 78–87, and compare it with the previous studies there referred to, will see that this was no mere lucky guess; but was led up to by a chain of close reasoning, such as gives us the highest confidence in the results and methods of Assyriology, at least in Professor Delitzsch's hands. He could not then have known of the discovery. The text was not published till October 1902.

When a man has been deeply immersed in an exacting study for many years he has a right to express opinions as well as to register facts. Whether the qualifications which make a man a successful investigator are always associated with those that enable a man to take a just view of the whole subject and its bearing upon other cognate subjects, may be doubted. But if the opinions do not coincide with those formed by others, with more or less acquaintance with the same facts, there is a fair field for discussion. It will be in the remembrance of most that some facts on which Professor Delitzsch relies for his positions have been used in the past to prove something very different.[1] In fact, if, as some of his opponents urge, his identifications do not hold, some of us will have to surrender some favourite bulwarks of the Old Testament. We seem to have a repetition of an old experience. Something is discovered which is first hailed as a remarkable confirmation of Scripture, then seen to be a serious impeachment of its accuracy, finally known to be purely independent and unconnected. It is an indirect testimony to the abiding value of the Hebrew Scriptures that the first question for most people concerning each new discovery is, How does it bear on the Bible?

Now, it is not an editor's function to reply to the arguments or opinions advanced in the work he edits, nor even to suppress and modify them, but to endeavour to place them as fairly as can be before the reader. A commentator might find it necessary to add

[1] Dr. S. Kinns' *Graven in the Rock,* Urquhart's *The Bible and Modern Discoveries,* Hommel's *Ancient Israelite Tradition.*

explanatory notes, supplementary information, or even references to other views. These are excluded by the plan of this work. Professor Delitzsch has acted as his own commentator, and in the notes will be found his replies to many critics and a fairly full list of the literature of the controversy. The great aim of this work is to let him speak for himself, and of this introduction to bespeak for him a fair hearing. Hence it must not be considered that this introduction pledges the editor to any view, for or against, any of the positions taken up in the work itself. Speculations as to his sympathies are disavowed in advance.

The worthy Professor somewhat pathetically complains that the public has hitherto taken but little note of the work done by scholars on the Old Testament. His lecture has had the result of attracting public notice enough. Not to speak of editions up to 40,000, replies already in a ninth edition, and a whole literature to itself, *Babel und Bibel* is now a historic event. Whether such publicity brings joy to the scholar may be doubted, but it is good for the public. Let us hope it may awaken interest in both Biblical study and Oriental exploration. Neither can afford to do without the other. Both need far more general support.

Some of the criticisms which the controversy has called forth perfectly dazzle our eyes to read. In an age when almost any argument is enough to base a popular cause upon, when men let themselves be led captive by the most specious nonsense, we are used to the publication of things as meaningless as the scrawlings of planchette. But even these meet with so much acceptance that they become a perilous influence on ill-regulated minds. Contemptuous silence is accepted as admission of doubt or lack of faith. Hence there is need for men who have knowledge to learn the art of making it available for public use.

One favourite device of the critics who have replied to Professor Delitzsch has been to fasten on some side issue. Often they attack

Assyriology as if that were the enemy. It was much the same when the New Learning came to pave the way for the Reformation, and Greek was regarded as an invention of the devil.

There are uncertainties, room for different opinions, in Assyriology, as there were doubts about Greek, some of which still remain. But some of the statements about Assyriology are so misleading as to call for vigorous treatment. Thus one reads that inasmuch as the cuneiform script employs some 20,000 sign groups and about 600 single signs, while the Hebrew has but 37 signs, there must be a wide field for uncertainty. The numbers are scarcely accurate. Brünnow's *Classified Sign List* only shews 13,000 sign groups, many of which are single signs, and 410 single signs, some of which are numerals. That each sign has many forms, according to the age of the script, may perhaps be the source of the confusion. But we do not count Old English, Gothic, and all the modern sorts of type as separate signs.

Even granting the numbers to be correct, what follows? One might as well object that since in Algebra a sign may denote any quantity whatever, even such as have no real value, therefore no Algebraical result was of numerical value. All depends upon the laws of combination and operation to which they are subjected. Provided all the signs are known in value, or obey such laws that their value can be readily deduced, their number is no hindrance, but rather a help. The vaunted simplicity of the 37 Hebrew signs is delusive. If they are so readily confounded one with another as textual critics suggest when they emend their texts, one may sigh for 20,000 unmistakable sign groups. Even if they are certain, what reliance can be placed on a script that uses the same signs to write Babel, Bible, and "babble"? All depends on knowing how the vowels, accents, etc., may be supplied. The cuneiform writes its vowels in full, even marking their length in many cases. Of course, an inscription may be so injured by erasure or exposure as to be almost illegible. So may a manuscript be. But here is the contrast. If an inscription is really legible its reading is easier, and more certain, than that of any manuscript unvocalized. Who shall say the vocalization is correct in the latter case? At any rate it is a late tradition.

When once an inscription is read, there may be lexical and grammatical difficulties. These are not unknown in Hebrew; they are more numerous than many, even good scholars, suspect. That men are conventionally agreed as to the sense of so many words in the Old Testament is often a disguised admission of the smallness of their knowledge. It may be perfect within the limits of their literature, but it is circumscribed by the limits of that literature. That men are still uncertain of the meaning of so many Hebrew words, after an infinitely larger amount of study bestowed on the language, is a warning to them to adopt fresh methods. That they have anything to teach a science, which by the labour of a few score men, for the most part unendowed with great means or much leisure for the pursuit of their study, has already attained a greater degree of certainty, is a contention not likely to be long maintained. The test for the unbiassed is to acquire an elementary acquaintance with the subject.

Uncertainty there is, and always must be, about the reading of defaced or fragmentary inscriptions. But the continual discovery of duplicates, which preserve entire lost portions of earlier known inscriptions; the immense amount of material, perhaps 100,000 tablets in the British Museum alone; the habit cuneiform scribes had of using various ways of writing the same word, a habit which constantly settles and confirms old readings; the fact that we have now plenty of bilinguals, giving renderings of cuneiform in Aramaic and Greek letters, not one of which has unsettled a reading hitherto accepted; place the results of cuneiform research in a much stronger position than any which could be deduced from a series of inscriptions in any mere Semitic alphabet. The only sensible course, then, for a man who doubts the results is to learn how they are obtained, and, if possible, check the process of deduction. He will find that the period of guesswork is over, and that decipherment is now a matter of the strictest logic.

That all results are unimpeachable is not true, for such things as *hapax legomena* occur, or phrases which by their invariable context, though often repeated, may be without the elucidation given by a more extended use in a variety of contexts. But, ever and anon, fresh texts present these words or phrases in fresh connections, and something of the old uncertainty gets shaded off, if not entirely removed. But, as a rule, in the historical texts the language is capable of a more minute grammatical analysis than can be safely applied to Hebrew, Aramaic, or Phœnician inscriptions. The more technical texts, astronomical or astrological, omens, magical or medical, are obscure, mainly because the subject itself is remote from our comprehension.

Much of the present security of cuneiform research is due to Professor Delitzsch. Long a teacher of beginners and a compiler of lexicons and grammar, he was always setting in order the foundations. Only lately has he begun to build upon them. Here, perhaps, it will turn out that he has not displayed sufficient caution. Those will come off best who try to shew that different conclusions may be drawn from his facts. They will not be well advised to quarrel with the facts. How dangerous that may be is seen by the humiliating position in which Professor P. Jensen has placed himself.[1] It does not do even for one of the foremost of Assyriologists to assume that he knows all there is behind Professor Delitzsch's assertions. In a formal treatise one demands full proof; in a lecture what is sometimes called the method of English scholarship is demanded, as contrasted with that of Germany, namely, a clear

[1] See p. 143, Notes.

dogmatic statement of results, rather than an exhibition of the machinery and process by which they are reached. In a first presentation of results the so-called German method is preferable. We want to see how they are obtained and so estimate their soundness. In a popular lecture this method is excluded. Few, if any, could attempt it: fewer follow it. What is needed is a clear statement of results and an avoidance of matters of doubtful interpretation. For a modest statement of facts it would be difficult to surpass this lecture. The deductions are subject to revision as more facts are taken into account. But it will not do to assume that the Professor has done a "bit of special pleading" and used up all the facts that suit his view, while leaving others ignored. The Professor could easily swell his list of facts manyfold, and, if he cannot lay his hand on them at once, there are many others who can. Anyone who desires to traverse his position successfully must be prepared with an alternative theory, which will not only fit all the facts adduced, but innumerable others of the same kind.

The explanation that men in similar circumstances hit upon similar devices, and thus reach similar institutions, is true enough. But it has not much point when the actual contacts between Babylonia and the people of Israel are considered. The fundamental assumption that the evolution of religious ideas went on in an orderly sequence in Israel, an assumption used to date the documents, is rudely shaken by the reflection that many ideas may have been adopted from Babylon and that the order of development there was not a synchronous order. Much that has been regarded as Persian in origin may turn out to be older than Abraham. But with such questions we have not to do here, only to note that they explain the antipathy of a school which might have been expected to welcome Delitzsch's work. One thing is certain, the opponent who appeals to authority, whether of the early Church or of the recent critic, will meet short shrift. If these lectures are to be answered the Professor must be met on his own ground, and that with better knowledge of cuneiform than most of his critics have shewn. The men who know have either preserved a discreet silence or gently chided him for some immaterial side issue. If the theologians are in future to deal successfully with such attacks on cherished positions, they must learn, and make provision for the teaching of Assyriology. They must include it in their curriculum.

The men who claim to decide everything by their own mother-wit have condemned the Professor and tried to influence the public by an appeal to sentiment and prejudice. We wish that the man, his facts and his conclusions, should have a patient hearing. The lectures will at least be found free of the ill-natured gibes at us which pass for wit with some of his critics. There is no need to swallow everything whole, nor to toss the Bible on the shelf as antiquated rubbish. If the Bible owes much to Babylonia, so do astronomy, mathematics, and medicine. We use still the Babylonian time measures and perhaps also their space measures. The debt of Greece and Rome to Babylon has yet to find its Delitzsch, but he is soon to appear.

Much has been made of the pain which comes to those who see old beliefs perish. But that is salutary pain. We have all to take pains, or pain. Either we must learn, research, investigate, deduce, conclude, or, if we will not take such pains, we are liable at any time to suffer pain from finding some cherished belief perish, without our being able to defend it, or even give it decent obsequies. As Dr. Kinns of old said, when he had proved to his satisfaction that the ark did not really harbour lions and tigers (in which he proved more a destructive critic than Professor Delitzsch), "It may seem a little too bad to deprive pictures and children's toys of this interesting feature, but there is strong evidence . . . ."; so when there is strong evidence we can only feel pity for those who have believed many things on evidence no better than that which justificd the lions and tigers. Whether Dr. Delitzsch has produced strong evidence or not is not for the editor to decide. That would be to step into the shoes of the artist and the toymaker. It is the object of this work to enable the reader to judge for himself. Men really must learn to have opinions of their own.

They accepted what they were told as babies. As men they need to put away childish things. They are babes still if they accept what is told them with no more effort to examine and verify. To throw aside all, and henceforth believe nothing, is as childish as before. To such adult infants this book may give the elements of an education such as they sorely need. If their so-called faith be unsettled, a very little more education will very likely settle it again; or, which comes to much the same thing with this sort of faith, they will forget all about it and believe as much or as little as before, the same things or something else, with equal complacency. The men of deep religious faith, who alone count for the progress of the race, will rejoice and take courage at a fresh proof that the Father has never left Himself without witness among men, and that even the most unlikely elements have gone to prepare the world for Him who was, and still is, to come.

C. H. W. JOHNS.

QUEENS' COLLEGE, CAMBRIDGE,
6th April 1903.

Babel and Bible

PREFACE TO LECTURE I

In spite of a conscientious examination of the rejoinders and critiques called forth by "Babel und Bibel," with the exception of certain improvements which for the most part aim at greater clearness and the avoidance of ambiguity, I have not found myself called upon to alter the actual contents. The notes appended to this new edition prove this as far as the most important of my statements are concerned.

LECTURE I

WHAT is the object of these labours in distant, inhospitable, and dangerous lands? To what

Fig. 1.—From the German excavations at Babylon.

end this costly work of rummaging in mounds many thousand years old, of digging deep down into the earth in places where no gold or silver is to be found? Why this rivalry among nations for the purpose of securing, each for itself, these desolate hills—and the more the better—in which to excavate? And from what source, on the other hand, is derived the

Fig. 2.—From the German excavations at Babylon.

self-sacrificing interest, ever on the increase, that is shewn on both sides of the ocean, in the excavations in Babylonia and Assyria?

To either question there is one answer, which, if not exhaustive, nevertheless to a great extent tells us the cause and aim: it is *the Bible.* The names Nineveh and Babylon, the stories of Belshazzar, and of the Wise Men who came from the East, have been surrounded, from our childhood up, by a mysterious charm; and however important the long lines of rulers whom we awaken anew to life may be in their bearings on history and civilization, they would not arouse half the amount of interest, were not Amraphel and Sennacherib and Nebuchadnezzar, who are familiar to us from our school-days, included among them. With these recollections of our childhood, however, is associated in riper years the struggle for a conception of the world which shall satisfy equally the understanding and the heart—a struggle which in the present day occupies the mind of every thinking man. And this leads us back again and again to the Bible, primarily to questions concerning the origin and meaning of the Old Testament, with which, however, the New is, from a historical point of view, inseparably linked. It is astonishing to what an extent the Old Testament, that small library of books of the most multifarious kind, is being investigated in every direction at the present day, by an almost inconceivable number of Christian scholars in Germany, England, and America—the three Bible-lands, as they have not unjustly been called. The public still continues to take but little notice of this quiet intellectual work. But this at least is certain, when once the sum-total of the new lessons that have been learnt has broken out of the study, and has come forth into life, into the church and into the school, the life of men and of peoples will be more deeply stirred, will be led on to more important advances than by the most noteworthy discoveries in the whole domain of Natural Science. At the same time, however, the conviction is becoming more and more general that it is the results of the excavations in Babylonia and Assyria in particular that are destined to inaugurate a new epoch as regards both the way in which we must understand the Old Testament and the estimate we must form of it, and that for all future time Babel and the Bible will remain closely connected.

The times have indeed changed! We had David, Solomon, 1000 B.C., Moses, 1400 B.C., and Abraham eight centuries earlier; and even detailed information about all these men! The thing seemed so unique, so supernatural, that the stories from the early beginnings of the world and of mankind were likewise accepted as credible—even great minds came under the spell of the mystery surrounding the first book of Moses. Now that the Pyramids have opened and the Assyrian palaces have disclosed themselves to view, the people of Israel with their writings appear one of the youngest among their neighbours.

Until far into the last century the Old Testament formed a world by itself; it spoke of times to whose latest limits the age of Classical Antiquity only just reaches, and of peoples of whom there is no mention or only a passing reference among Greek and Roman writers. From about 550 B.C. onwards, the Bible was the only source for the history of the Nearer East, and, since its range of vision spreads over the whole of the great quadrilateral between the Mediterranean and the Persian Gulf, from Ararat to Ethiopia, it is full of problems the solution of which would never perhaps have been successfully achieved. Now, at a stroke, the walls that have shut off the remoter portion of the Old Testament scene of action fall, and a cool quickening breeze from the East, accompanied by a flood of light, breathes through and illuminates the whole of the time-honoured Book—all the more intensely because Hebrew antiquity from beginning to end is closely linked with this same Babylonia and Assyria.

The American excavations in Nippur have brought to light the business records of the great commercial firm of Murashû & Sons,[1] which was established there in the time of Artaxerxes (about 450 B.C.). In these records we find the names of many Jewish exiles who remained in Babylon—Nathanael, Haggai, Benjamin. And in connection with the

[1] See Note, p. 92.

city of Nippur we read also of a canal *Kabar*; in which the canal Chebar "in the land of the Chaldeans," famous on account of Ezekiel's vision (Ezek. i. 3) is recovered. This Grand Canal—for that is the meaning of the name—may even survive to the present day.

As the Babylonian bricks nearly always bear a stamp, mentioning, among other details, the name of the city to which the building in question belonged, Sir Henry Rawlinson, as far back as 1849, succeeded in discovering the long-sought city of Ur of the Chaldees, in several passages attested as the home of Abraham, *i.e.*, the tribal ancestors of Israel (Gen. xi. 31, xv. 7)—at el-Muḳayyar, the mighty mound of ruins on the right-hand bank of the lowest course of the Euphrates (fig. 3). The statements in the cuneiform literature on geographical matters are so clear, that though the city of Carchemish, where Nebuchadnezzar in 605 B.C. obtained his great victory over Pharaoh Necho (Jer. xlvi. 2) was previously sought, now in one place, now in another, on the banks of the Euphrates, the English Assyriologist George Smith, in March 1876, rode direct from Aleppo down the stream from Birejik, to the district where, according to the cuneiform inscriptions, the old Hittite royal

Fig. 3.—The ruins of el-Muḳayyar (Ur of the Chaldees).

city must have lain, and at once, with the greatest certainty, identified the ruins of *Jerabis*—greater than Nineveh, with walls and palace-mounds—with Carchemish, an identification immediately afterwards confirmed by the inscriptions in that peculiar Hittite hieroglyphic script (fig. 4) which were found scattered among the ruins.

And as is the case with a large number of the places, so also many of the personages named in the Bible now receive colour and life. The book of Isaiah (xx. 1) mentions, on

Fig. 4.—Hittite hieroglyphs from Carchemish.

one occasion, an Assyrian king named Sargon who had sent his field-marshal against Ashdod. When in 1843 the French consul Emile Botta began to dig at Khorsabad, the ruined mound not far from Mosul, and thus at the advice of a German scholar inaugurated archæological researches in Mesopotamian soil, the very first Assyrian palace to be discovered was that of this Sargon, the conqueror of Samaria. Upon

Fig. 5.—Sargon II. and his field-marshal.

one of the magnificent alabaster reliefs with which the walls of the palace chambers were adorned, the very person of this mighty warrior conversing with his field-marshal meets our gaze (fig. 5). The Book of Kings (2 Kings

xviii. 14 *sqq.*) relates that King Sennacherib, in the south Palestinian city of Lachish, received the tribute of King Hezekiah of Jerusalem. A relief from Sennacherib's palace in Nineveh

Fig. 6.—King Ḫammurabi (Amraphel).

shews us the Assyrian monarch, enthroned before his tent, facing a conquered city, and the accompanying inscription states that "Sennacherib the king of the universe, king of Asshur, seated himself on his throne and inspected the spoil of Lachish." And Sennacherib's Babylonian adversary, Merodach-baladan, in his turn—who, according to the Bible (2 Kings xx. 12), sent messengers of peace to Hezekiah—is shewn us upon a fine diorite-relief now at Berlin: before the king stands the governor of Babylon, to whom his royal master in

Fig. 7.—Seal of Darius Hystaspis.

his graciousness has presented large estates. Even the great king Ḫammurabi—Amraphel (Gen. xiv.)—the contemporary of Abraham, is now pictorially represented (*e.g.* fig. 6). Thus, all the men who throughout three thousand years made the history of the world, come to life again; even their seal-cylinders have survived. Here we have the seal of King

Darius, the son of Hystaspis (fig. 7):—the king lion-hunting under the august protection of Ahuramazda, with the inscription at the side in three languages: "I am Darius the great king"—a veritable treasure belonging to the British Museum. Here (fig. 8) the state-seal of Sargani-šar-ali, or Sargon I., one of the oldest of

Fig. 8.—Seal of Sargon I.

the Babylonian rulers yet known, of the third, probably even the fourth, millennium B.C. This is the king who caused the legend to be related of him that he knew not his father—for he died before his birth—and that his widowed mother, as his father's brother shewed no care for her,[1] brought him into the world in great distress: "in Azupiran on the

[1] See Note, p. 92.

Euphrates she secretly gave birth to me, put me in a little ark of reeds, closed the opening with bitumen, laid me in the river, that bore me down on its waves to Akki, the water-carrier. In the benevolence of his heart he took me in, brought me up as his child, made me his gardener. Then Ishtar, the daughter of the King of Heaven, conceived an affection for me and raised me up to be king over men."

But even whole nations come to life again. When we collect the various ethnical types[1] from the Assyrian sculptures, and fix our eyes in one case upon the representation of a Judæan from Lachish (fig. 11), and in another upon an Israelite of the time of Jehu (fig. 10), it suggests itself as likely that the other types also—*e.g.* the Elamite chieftain (9), the Arab rider (13), and the Babylonian merchant (12)—have been accurately observed and reproduced. In particular, the Assyrians, who but six decades ago seemed to have been swallowed up, together with their history and

[1] See Note, p. 93.

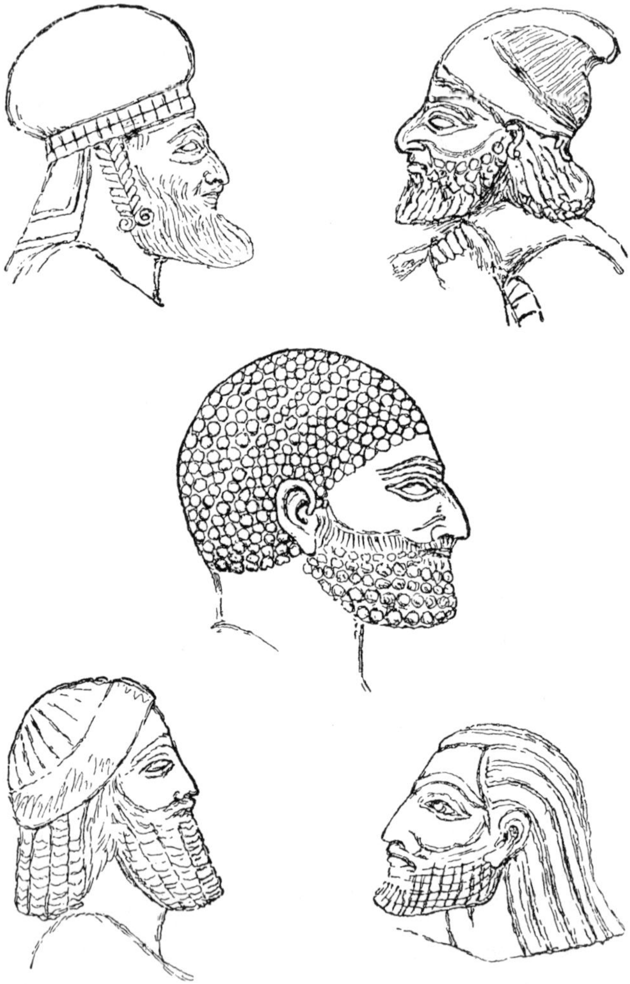

9. Elamite.
12. Babylonian.
11. Judæan.
10. Israelite.
13. Arab.

culture, in the stream of ages, are now known to us through the excavations in Nineveh to the minutest details, and many passages in the prophetical books of the Old Testament receive vivid local colour.

"Behold, they shall come with speed swiftly. None shall be weary nor stumble among them; none shall slumber nor sleep; neither shall the girdle of their loins be loosed, nor the latchet of their shoes be broken: whose arrows are sharp, and all their bows bent, their horses' shoes shall be counted like flint, and their wheels like a whirlwind. Their roaring shall be like a lion, and they shall lay hold of the prey and shall carry it away safe, and none shall deliver it."

Thus does the prophet Isaiah (v. 26 *sqq.*) in eloquent language describe the Assyrian troops. Now we see these Assyrian soldiers setting out from the camp in the early morn (fig. 14), and with battering-rams assaulting the enemy's stronghold (fig. 15), whilst on the lower line of the relief unhappy captives are being con-

Fig. 14.—Departure of Assyrian troops from the camp.

Fig. 15.—Assault upon an Assyrian fortress with battering-rams.

ducted on the journey from which there is no return. We see (fig. 16) the Assyrian archers and spearmen hurling their missiles at the hostile fortress, and, elsewhere, Assyrian warriors storming a hill which is defended by the enemy's archers: they draw themselves up to the branches of trees or climb up

Fig. 16.—Assyrian archers and spearmen.

with the help of staffs, whilst others are triumphantly carrying down to the valley the severed heads of the enemy. Thanks to a number of these war-pictures on the bronze gates of Shalmaneser II., as well as on the alabaster reliefs from the palaces of Sargon and Sennacherib, the war-methods of this the first military state in the world, down to the details of arms and equipment and their gradual improvement, are made known to us.

Fig. 17.—Assyrian staff-officer of Sargon II.

Here (fig. 17) is the representation of one of Sargon's Assyrian staff-officers, whose beard is

Fig. 18.—Pages in ceremonial procession.

dressed with a skill that has not yet been attained even by our officers of to-day. Here are the pages of the royal household making

Fig. 19.—Pages bearing the royal chariot.

Fig. 20.—Pages bearing the royal throne.

Fig. 21.—King Ashur-bani-pal at the hunt.

their ceremonial entrance (fig. 18), bearing the royal chariot (fig. 19), or the royal throne (fig. 20). Many beautiful reliefs shew us King Sardanapalus (Ashur-bani-pal) out hunting (fig. 21), especially when engaged in his favourite sport, the hunting of lions, of which

Fig. 22.—Ashur-bani-pal lion-hunting on horseback.

a number of remarkably fine specimens were always kept ready for the day of the hunt in a park specially reserved for game.

When King Saul was unwilling to allow the youthful David to set out to fight against Goliath, David reminded him that many a time whilst shepherding his father's flock,

Fig. 23.—Ashur-bani-pal hunts the lions from a chariot.

Fig. 24.—Ashur-bani-pal fighting the lion on foot.

when a lion or bear carried off an animal, he had gone out after it, had smitten it, and wrested from it the prey; and when the lion had turned against him he had caught it by its

Figs. 25, 26.—Preparations for the royal table.

beard and killed it. This was precisely the custom in Assyria. The reliefs, accordingly, shew us King Ashur-bani-pal in combat with a lion; and not only on horseback (fig. 22) and in a chariot (fig. 23); we also see the king of Asshur fighting at close quarters on foot (fig. 24), courageously measuring his strength with the king of the desert. We catch a glimpse of the preparations for the royal table (figs. 25, 26); we see servants carrying hares,

Fig. 27.—King and Queen in vine-encircled bower.

partridges, locusts attached to sticks, besides an abundance of cakes and fruits of all kinds, and holding a small green branch in one hand to keep off flies. Nay more, on a relief from the harem (fig. 27) we are even permitted to see the king and queen refreshing themselves with choice wine in a vine-encircled bower: the king reclining upon a lofty couch, the queen, gorgeously robed, sitting opposite to

Fig. 28.—Wife of Ashur-bani-pal.

him upon a high chair; eunuchs are cooling them both with fans, whilst, from a distance, the music of stringed instruments falls upon their ears. It is the only extant representation of a queen, and her profile, much better preserved in former years, was rescued for posterity in 1867 by a drawing (fig. 28) made by a Prussian lieutenant, afterwards Colonel Billerbeck. It is quite possible that this consort of Ashur-bani-pal was a princess of Aryan blood, and may be imagined with fair hair.

Fig. 29.—Procession of gods.

And much else in Assyrian antiquity that may interest us is pictorially presented to our gaze. The prophet Isaiah (xlv. 20, xlvi. 1) mentions processions of gods[1]; here (fig. 29) we see a procession of the kind: the goddesses in front, behind them the thunder-god armed with hammer and a sheaf of thunderbolts, whilst Assyrian soldiers have been ordered to

[1] See Note, p. 93.

carry the images of the gods. We see how the heavy colossal bulls were moved from place to place (fig. 30), and at the same time get glimpses of every kind into the technical accomplishments of the Assyrians. But above

Fig. 30.—The conveying of a colossal bull.

all we may revel again and again in the noble style of their architecture, noble in its simplicity, as shewn to us in the gate of Sargon's palace (fig. 31), excavated by Botta, and we may revel equally in the fine animal-representations, full of the most striking realism, which those "Dutch Masters" of antiquity have created, as, for example, the idyl of the peacefully grazing antelopes (fig. 32), or the dying lioness from

Fig. 31.—Gate of Sargon's palace.

Fig. 32.—Grazing antelopes.

Nineveh famed in the annals of art (fig. 33). The excavations on Babylonian soil also open up to us in exactly the same way the art and culture of this the mother-country of Assyrian civilization, taking us as far back as the fourth millennium, that is to say, to times which the boldest imagination could never have dreamed

Fig. 33.—The dying lioness from Nineveh.

of reaching again. We penetrate into the age of the Sumerians, that primæval race, neither Indo-germanic nor Semitic, whose people were the creators and founders of the great Babylonian civilization, and to whom the number sixty (not a hundred) represented the next higher unit after the ten. The Sumerian chief-priest, whose magnificently preserved head (fig. 34) is in the Berlin Museum, may certainly be described as a noble representative of the human race at the dawn of history.

Yet, however instructive and deserving of

Fig. 34.—Head of a high priest.

recognition all these features may be, they are but details and, so to say, externals, such as are easily surpassed in importance by the facts now to be mentioned.

I am not thinking here of the circumstance, of eminent value though it be, that the Babylonian-Assyrian chronology, with its strictly astronomical basis—the observation of eclipses of the sun, etc.—now allows us to arrange chronologically and in a systematic manner the events recorded in the biblical books of the Kings (a result for which we should be doubly thankful, since Robertson Smith and Wellhausen have proved that the Old Testament chronology is conformed to a system of sacred numbers: 480 years from the end of the Exile back to the Founding of the Temple of Solomon, and again 480 years [see 1 Kings vi. 1] from the Founding of the Temple to the Exodus of the Children of Israel from Egypt). Even the far-reaching importance which cuneiform research has had for the increasingly better understanding of the text of the Old Testament (thanks to the remarkably close relationship subsisting between the Babylonian and Hebrew languages and to the vast extent of the Babylonian literature) can here be illustrated by just one simple example: "The Lord bless thee and keep thee: The Lord make his face shine upon thee, and be gracious unto thee: The Lord lift up his countenance upon thee, and give thee peace." How many times, times without number, is this threefold blessing (Num. vi. 24 *sqq.*) spoken and heard! Yet its meaning has only come to be realized by us in all its profundity now that the Babylonian usage has taught us that "to lift up his face, his eyes, upon or to one" is a particularly favourite expression used of the deity who "bestows his pleasure, his love, upon a chosen man (or place)."[1] The sublime blessing, accordingly, asking more and more as it proceeds, craves for man from God blessing and protection, friendliness and grace, and finally, even God's love, closing with the words, "Peace be with thee," that truly beautiful Eastern greeting, of which Friedrich Rückert, inspired by a verse in the Koran, sings:

When ye enter any house
  "Peace be with you" shall ye say;
"Peace be yours" ye shall repeat
  Ere ye turn your steps away.
Men have uttered many a prayer,
None has breathed a word more fair
  Than "Peace be here below."

[1] See Note, p. 94.

But even the great help which Babylon unexpectedly brings to the philological understanding of the Bible must, as regards importance, be assigned a second place in view of the considerations that follow.

One of the most notable results of the archæological researches on the Euphrates and Tigris is the discovery that in the Babylonian lowland, a district of about the size of Italy, which nature had already made uncommonly fruitful, but which human energy converted into a hothouse of vegetation passing our conception, there existed as early as about 2250 B.C.[1] a highly-developed constitution, together with a state of culture that may well be compared with that of our later Middle Ages. After Ḫammurabi had succeeded in driving out of the country the Elamites, the hereditary foes of Babylonia, and had amalgamated the north and south of the land into one united state, with Babylon as the political and religious centre, his first care was to enforce uniform laws throughout the land. He therefore pre-

[1] See Note, p. 96.

pared a great code which defined the civil law in all its branches. In this code, the relations of master to slave and labourer, of merchant to agent, of landed proprietor to tenant-farmer, are strictly regulated. There is a law to the effect that the agent who pays over money to his principal for goods sold must receive a receipt from the latter; abatement of rent is provided for in the event of damage by storm or flood; fishing-rights for each village situated on a canal are accurately defined, etc. Babylon is the seat of the supreme court, to which all difficult and contested lawsuits have to be referred for decision. Every able man is bound to serve as a soldier, although Ḫammurabi took precautions against a too excessive use of conscription, by means of numerous decrees, recognising the privileges of the old priestly families, or exempting shepherds from military service in the interests of cattle-breeding.

We read of writing in Babylon; and the extremely cursive nature of the writing points to the widest application of it. In truth, when we find, among the letters which have survived from those ancient times in great abundance, the letter of a woman to her husband on his travels, wherein, after telling him that the little ones are well, she asks advice on some trivial matter; or the missive of a son to his father, in which he informs him that so-and-so has mortally offended him, that he would thrash the knave, but would like to ask his father's advice first; or another letter in which a son urges his father to send at last the long-promised money, offering the insolent inducement that then he will pray for his father again — all this points to a well-organised system of communication by letter and of postal arrangements, and shews, also, to judge by all the indications, that streets, bridges, and canals, even beyond the frontiers of Babylon, were in excellent condition.

Trade and commerce, cattle-breeding and agriculture, were at their prime, and the sciences, *e.g.* geometry, mathematics, and, above all, astronomy, had reached a degree of development which again and again moves even the astronomers of to-day to admiration and astonishment. Not Paris, at the outside Rome, can compete with Babylon in respect of the influence which it exercised upon the

Fig. 35.—The Babylon of Nebuchadnezzar (restored).

world throughout two thousand years. The Prophets of the Old Testament attest in terms full of displeasure the overpowering grandeur and overwhelming might of the Babylon of Nebuchadnezzar (fig. 35). "A golden cup," exclaims Jeremiah (li. 7), "was Babylon in the hand of Yahwè, which hath made the whole earth drunken"; and even down to the time of the Apocalypse of John, words are found which quiver with the hateful memory of the great Babel, the luxurious, gay city, the wealth-abounding centre of trade and art, the mother of harlots and of every abomination upon earth. And this focus of culture and science and literature, the 'brain' of the Nearer East, and the all-ruling power, was the city of Babylon, even at the close of the third millennium.

It was in the winter of 1887 that Egyptian fellaḥîn digging for antiquities at El-Amarna, the ruins of the royal city of Amenophis IV., between Thebes and Memphis, found there some three hundred clay-tablets of all sizes. These tablets are, as has since been shewn, the letters of Babylonian, Assyrian, and Mesopotamian kings to the Pharaohs Amenophis III. and IV., and especially the written communications of Egyptian governors from the great Canaanite cities, such as Tyre, Sidon, Acco, Ascalon, to the Egyptian court; and the Berlin Museums are fortunate enough to possess the only letters from Jerusalem, written even before the immigration of the Israelites into the promised land. Like a mighty reflector, this discovery of clay-tablets at Amarna has turned into a dazzling light the deep darkness which lay over the Mediterranean lands—Canaan in particular—and over their politics and culture at about 1500–1400 B.C. And the fact alone that all these chiefs of Canaan, and even of Cyprus, avail themselves of the Babylonian writing and language, and write on clay-tablets like the Babylonians, that, therefore, the Babylonian tongue was the official language of diplomatic intercourse from the Euphrates to the Nile, proves the all-ruling influence of the Babylonian culture and literature from 2200 to beyond 1400 B.C.

When, therefore, the twelve tribes of Israel invaded Canaan, they came to a land which was a domain completely pervaded by Babylonian culture.[1] It is a small but characteristic

[1] See Note, p. 97.

feature that, on the conquest and despoiling of the first Canaanite city, Jericho, a *Babylonish* mantle excited the greed of Achan (Josh. vii. 21). Yet it was not only the commerce, but also the trade, law, custom, and science of Babylon that set the fashion in the land. Thus we can at once understand why, for example, the coinage, the system of weights and measures, the outward forms of the law—"if a man does so and so, he shall so and so"—are precisely Babylonian, and just as the sacrificial and priestly system of the Old Testament is profoundly influenced by the Babylonian, so it is significant that Israelite tradition itself no longer affords any certain information respecting the origin of the Sabbath (*cf.* Exod. xx. 11 with Deut. v. 15).

But since the Babylonians also had a Sabbath day (*šabattu*),[1] on which, for the purpose of conciliating the gods, there was a festival—that is to say, no work was to be done—and since the seventh, fourteenth,

[1] See Note, p. 98.

twenty-first, and twenty-eighth days of a month are marked on a calendar of sacrifices and festivals dug up in Babylonia as days on which "the shepherd of the great nations" shall eat no roast flesh, shall not change his dress, shall not offer sacrifice, as days on which the king shall not mount the chariot, or pronounce judgment, the Magus shall not prophesy, even the physician shall not lay his hand on the sick, in short, as days which "are not suitable for any affair (business ?)," it is scarcely possible for us to doubt that we owe the blessings decreed in the Sabbath or Sunday day of rest in the last resort to that ancient and civilized race on the Euphrates and Tigris.

Nay, even more! The Berlin Museums have in their keeping a particularly valuable treasure. It consists of a clay-tablet with a Babylonian legend which tells how it happened that the first man came to forfeit immortality. The place where this tablet was found—viz., El-Amarna—and the many dots in red Egyptian ink found in different places all over the tablet (shewing the pains the Egyptian scholar had taken to make the foreign text intelligible), give ocular proof how eagerly the works of Babylonian literature were studied even at that ancient date in lands as far away as that of the Pharaohs. Is it surprising, then, that the same thing should have happened in Palestine also in earlier as well as in later days, and that now, all at once, a series of Biblical narratives come to us in their original form from the Babylonian treasure-mounds, rising, as it were, out of the night into the light of day?

The Babylonians divided their history into two great periods: the one before, the other after the Flood. Babylon was in quite a peculiar sense the land of deluges. The alluvial lowlands along the course of all great rivers discharging into the sea are, of course, exposed to terrible floods of a special kind—cyclones and tornadoes accompanied by earthquakes and tremendous downpours of rain.

As late as the year 1876, a tornado of this

kind coming from the Bay of Bengal, accompanied by fearful thunder and lightning, and blowing with such force that ships at a distance of 300 kilometres (nearly 190 miles) were dismasted, approached the mouths of the Ganges, and the high cyclonic waves, uniting with the then ebbing tide, formed one gigantic tidal wave, with the result that within a short while an area of 141 geographical square miles was covered with water to a depth of 45 feet, and 215,000 men met their death by drowning. The storm raged in this way until the flood spent itself on the higher ground. When we reflect upon this, we can estimate what a frightful catastrophe a cyclone of the kind must have meant when it came upon the lowlands of Babylon in those primæval days. It is the merit of the celebrated Viennese geologist Eduard Suess to have shewn that there is an accurate description of such a cyclone, line for line, in the Babylonian Deluge-story written upon a tablet (see fig. 36) from the Library of Sardanapalus at Nineveh, of which, however, a written account had existed as early as 2000 B.C. The sea plays the chief part in the story, and the ship of Xisuthros, the Babylonian Noah,

Fig. 36.—Tablet with the Deluge-story.

is accordingly cast upon a spur of the mountain-range of Armenia and Media; in other respects, however, it is the Deluge-story so well known to us all. Xisuthros receives a command from the god of the ocean depths to build a ship of a specified size, to pitch it thoroughly, and to embark upon it his family and all living seed; the party go on board ship, its doors are closed, it is thrust out into the all-destroying billows until at length it strands upon a mountain called Nizir. Then follows the famous passage: "On the seventh day I brought out a dove and released it; the dove flew hither and thither, but as there was no resting-place it returned again." We then read further how that the swallow was released and returned again, until, finally, the raven, finding that the waters had subsided, returned not again to the ship, and how that Xisuthros leaves the vessel, and offers upon the top of the mountain a sacrifice, the sweet savour whereof is smelt by the gods, and so on. The whole story, precisely as it was written down, travelled to Canaan.[1] But owing to the new and entirely different local conditions, it was forgotten that the sea was the chief factor, and so we find in the Bible two accounts of

[1] See Note, p. 102.

the Deluge, which are not only scientifically impossible, but, furthermore, mutually contradictory—the one assigning to it a duration of 365 days, the other of $[40+(3\times 7)]=61$ days. Science is indebted to Jean Astruc, that strictly orthodox Catholic physician of Louis XIV., for recognising that two fundamentally different accounts of a deluge have been worked up into a single story in the Bible. In the year 1753, Astruc, as Goethe expresses it, first "applied the knife and probe to the Pentateuch," and thereby became the founder of the criticism of the Pentateuch—that is to say, of the study which perceives more and more clearly the very varied written sources from which the five Books of Moses have been compiled. These are facts that, as far as science is concerned, stand firm and remain unshaken, however tightly people on either side of the ocean may continue to close their eyes to them. When we reflect that in time past the Copernican system was offensive even to such men of genius as Luther and Melanchthon, we must be quite prepared to find only a tardy recognition of the results of Pentateuchal criticism; but the course of time will surely bring with it light.

The ten Babylonian antediluvian kings also have been admitted into the Bible, and figure as the ten antediluvian patriarchs, with various points of agreement as to details.

Besides the Babylonian epic of Gilgamesh, the eleventh tablet of which gives the Deluge-story, we also possess another beautiful Babylonian poem: the creation-epic,[1] written upon seven tablets. At the very beginning of all things, according to this story, a dark, chaotic, primæval water, called Tiâmat, existed in a state of agitation and tumult. But as soon as the gods made preparations for the formation of an ordered universe, Tiâmat, generally represented as a dragon, but also as a seven-headed serpent, arose in bitter enmity, gave birth to monsters of all kinds—in particular, gigantic serpents filled with venom—and with these as her allies, prepared, roaring and

[1] See Note, p. 104.

snorting, to do battle with the gods. All the gods tremble with fear when they perceive their terrible adversary; only the god Marduk, the god of light, the god of the early morning and of spring, volunteered to do battle on condition that the first place among the gods be conceded to him. A splendid scene follows. The god Marduk fastens a mighty net to the east and south, north and west, in order that nothing of Tiâmat may escape; then clad in gleaming armour, and in majestic splendour, he mounts his chariot drawn by four fiery steeds, the gods around gazing with admiration. Straight he drives to meet the dragon and her army, and utters the call to single combat. Then Tiâmat uttered wild and piercing cries until her ground quaked asunder from the bottom. She opened her jaws to their utmost, but before she could close her lips the god Marduk bade the evil wind enter within her, then seizing the javelin, he cut her heart in pieces, cast down her body and stood upon it, whilst her myrmidons were placed in durance vile. Then Marduk clave Tiâmat clean asunder like a fish; out of the one half he formed heaven, out of the other, earth, at the same time dividing the upper waters from the lower by means of the firmament; he decked the heavens with moon, sun and stars, the earth with plants and animals, until at length the first human pair, made of clay mingled with divine blood, went forth fashioned by the hand of the creator.

As Marduk was the tutelary deity of the city of Babel, we can readily believe that this narrative in particular became very widely diffused in Canaan. Indeed, the Old Testament poets and prophets even went so far as to transfer Marduk's heroic act directly to Yahwè, and thenceforth extolled him as being the one who in the beginning of time broke in pieces the heads of the sea-monster (*liviāthân*, Ps. lxxiv. 13 *sq.*; *cf.* lxxxix. 10), as the one through whom the helpers of the dragon (*râhâb*) were overthrown. Such passages as

Is. li. 9: "Awake, awake, put on strength, O arm of Yahwè! awake, as in the ancient days, the generations of old. Art thou not it that hewed the dragon in pieces, that pierced the monster (*tannîn*)?" or Job xxvi. 12: "By his strength he smote the sea, and by his wisdom he dashed in pieces the dragon," read like a commentary on that small representation of Marduk which was found by our expedition. The god is shewn to us clad in majestic glory, with mighty arm and large eye and ear, symbolic of his sagacity, and at his feet is the vanquished dragon of the primæval ocean (fig. 37). The priestly scholar who composed Gen. chap. i. endeavoured, of course, to remove all possible mythological features of this creation-story.[1] But the dark, watery chaos is presupposed, and that, too, with the name Tehôm (*i.e.* Tiâmat), and is first divided from the light, after which the heavens and the earth emerge. The heavens are furnished with sun, moon, and stars, the

[1] See Note, p. 104.

earth, clad with vegetation, is supplied with animals, and finally the first human pair come forth fashioned by the hand of God ; and this being so, the very close connection that exists

Fig. 37.—The god Marduk.

between the Biblical and the Babylonian creation stories is as clear and illuminating as are and always will be futile all attempts to bring our Biblical story of the creation into conformity with the results of Natural Science.[1] It is interesting to note that there is still an echo of this contest between Marduk and Tiâmat in the Apocalypse of John, where we read of a conflict between the Archangel Michael and the "Beast of the Abyss, the

Fig. 38.—The conflict with the Dragon.

Old Serpent, which is the Devil and Satan." The whole conception, also present in the story of the knight St. George and his conflict with the dragon, a story brought back by the Crusaders, is manifestly Babylonian. For fine reliefs (fig. 38), older by many centuries than

[1] See Note, p. 109.

the Apocalypse or the first chapter of Genesis, are found on the walls of the Assyrian palaces, representing the conflict between the power of light and the power of darkness, which is resumed with each new day, with every spring as it begins anew.

To recognise these connecting links is, however, of still greater importance.

The command not to do to one's neighbour what one does not wish to have done to one's self is indelibly stamped upon every human heart. "Thou shalt not shed thy neighbour's blood, thou shalt not approach thy neighbour's wife, thou shalt not seize upon thy neighbour's garment"—these requirements of fundamental importance for the self-preservation of human society are found, in the case of the Babylonians, in precisely the same connection as the fifth, sixth, and seventh commandments of the Old Testament. But man is also a being destined to live a social life, and on this account the social requirements—readiness to help, compassion, love—constitute an equally inalienable heritage of human nature. When, therefore, the Babylonian Magus, having been called in to see a patient, seeks to know what sins have thrown him thus upon the sick bed, he does not stop short at such gross sins of commission as murder or theft, but asks, "Have you failed to clothe a naked person, or to cause a prisoner to see the light?" The Babylonians laid stress even upon those postulates of human ethics which stand on a higher level; to speak the truth, to keep one's promise, seemed to them as sacred a duty as to say 'Yea' with the mouth and 'Nay' in the heart was, in their view, a punishable offence. It is not strange, therefore, that to the Babylonians, as to the Hebrews, transgressions against these commands and prohibitions present themselves in the character of sins; the Babylonians also felt themselves to be in every respect entirely dependent upon the gods.

It is even more noteworthy that they, too, regarded all human suffering, illness in particular, and finally death, as a punishment for

[1] See Note, p. 113.

sins. In Babel, as in the Bible, the sense of sin is the dominating force everywhere. Under these circumstances we can understand that Babylonian thinkers pondered over the problem: How it could have been possible for man, who had come forth into the world as the work of God's hand, and had been made after God's own likeness, to become the victim of sin and death. The Bible contains that beautiful and profound story of the corruption of the woman by the serpent — again the serpent? There is certainly quite a Babylonian ring about it! Was it perhaps that serpent, the earliest enemy of the gods, seeking to revenge itself upon the gods of light by alienating from them their noblest creation? Or was it that serpent-god, of whom in one place it is said "he destroyed the abode of life"? The problem as to the origin of the Biblical story of the Fall is second to none in significance, in its bearings on the history of religion, and above all for New Testament theology, which, as is well known, sets off against the first Adam, through whom sin and death came into the world, the second Adam. Perhaps we may be permitted to lift the veil a little. May we point to an old Babylonian cylinder-seal (fig. 39)? Here, in the middle, is the tree with hanging fruit; on the right the man, to be recognised by the horns, the symbol of strength, on the left the

Fig. 39.—Babylonian representation of the Fall.

woman; both reaching out their hands to the fruit, and behind the woman the serpent. Should there not be a connection between this old Babylonian representation and the Biblical story of the Fall?[1]

Man dies, but while his body is laid to rest in the grave, his soul separates from it and descends to the "land without return," to

[1] See Note, p. 114.

Sheol, Hades, the place, full of dust and gloom, where the Shades flutter about like birds, leading a dull and joyless existence: doors and bars are covered with dust, and everything in which the heart of man had once rejoiced has become dust and mould. With such a comfortless outlook we can easily understand that to the Hebrews, as to the Babylonians, length of days in this life seemed to be the highest of blessings. And so Marduk's procession street, unearthed by the German expedition in Babylon, is paved with large slabs of stone, on each of which is inscribed a prayer of Nebuchadnezzar's, concluding with the words: "O Lord Marduk, grant long life!" But this is remarkable: the Babylonian conception of the under-world is one degree, at any rate, more cheerful than that of the Old Testament. Upon the twelfth tablet of the Gilgamesh epic, which, so far, has only come down to us in fragments, the Babylonian under-world is described with the greatest precision. Here we read of a place within the confines of the under-world, evidently reserved for those who are pious in a special degree, "in which they (the pious) rest on couches and drink clear water." Many Babylonian coffins have been found in Warka, Nippur, and Babel. But the Department of the Berlin Museums for Antiquities of the Nearer East has recently acquired a small clay

Fig. 40.—Clay cone from a Babylonian coffin.

cone (fig. 40), which is obviously derived from a coffin of the kind, and whose inscription entreats, in touching terms, that whosoever shall find this coffin may leave it in its place and do it no injury, and the little text concludes with words of blessing for whosoever should act thus kindly: "may his name continue to be blessed in the world above; in the world below may his departed spirit drink clear water." In Sheol, therefore, there was a place for those who were perfectly pious, where they recline upon couches and drink clear water. Consequently, is it not probable that the rest of Sheol would be strictly reserved for the not-pious, and as it was not merely dusty but even waterless, or a place that supplied, at the best, "turbid water"—would it not, at all events, be a place of thirst? In the Book of Job, which betrays a close acquaintance with Babylonian views, we find (xxiv. 18 *sq.*) the contrast between a hot, waterless desert, destined for the wicked, and a garden, with clear, fresh water, for the pious.[1] In the New Testament, too, where this conception is mingled, in a curious manner, with the last verse of the Book of Isaiah, we actually read of a fiery hell, in which the rich man pants for water, and of a garden (Paradise) with plenty of clear, fresh water for Lazarus.[2] And how much has since

[1] See Note, p. 118. [2] See Note, p. 118.

been made of this hell and this Paradise by painters and poets, by the fathers of the church and priests, and finally by the prophet Mohammed, is sufficiently well known. Mark yonder poor Moslem who has been left behind by the caravan, weak and helpless in the desert, because he is no longer equal to the fatigues of the journey. A small cupful of water is at his side, he is digging with his own hand a shallow grave in the desert-sand, resignedly awaiting death. His eyes brighten, for but a little longer and the angels will come forth from the wide-opened gates of Paradise to greet him with the words: "*Selam alaika*, thou hast been pious, therefore enter now for ever into the Garden which Allah has assigned to those who are his." The garden is equal in extent to the heaven and the earth. Gardens decked with dense foliage, abounding in sheltered spots, and richly supplied with low-hanging fruits, are intersected on every side by brooks and springs, and bowers cooled by the breeze rise up on the banks of the rivers of Paradise. The lustre of Paradise is reflected in the faces of the blessed, beaming with joy and happiness. They wear green raiment of the finest silk and brocade. Their arms are adorned with gold and silver bracelets. They recline on couches provided with thick mattresses and soft cushions, and at their feet are soft rugs. Thus reclining face to face, they sit at luxuriously furnished tables, that afford whatsoever they desire. A well-supplied goblet is passed round, and youths endowed with immortality, looking like strewn pearls, make the circle with silver tankards and glass mugs filled with Maïn, the finest, clearest water, redolent of camphor and ginger, from the well of Tasnim, from which the archangels drink. And this water is mingled with the choicest of old wines, whereof they may drink as much as they will, since it makes not drunken and leaves no headache. Then, in addition to this, there are the Houris. Damsels with a skin as delicate as the ostrich egg, with heaving bosoms, and with eyes like pearls hidden in the shell, eyes like the gazelle's, full of modest yet heart-ensnaring glances. Seventy-two of these Houris may each of the blessed ones select in addition to the wives which he has had on earth, provided he desires to retain them (and the good man will always have good desires). All hatred and jealousy has vanished from the breast of the blessed; no gossip, no falseness is to be found in Paradise: "*Selam, selam*" rings out everywhere, and all speech dies away with the words: *el-ḥamdu lillâhi rabbi-l-ʿ âlamîn*, "praise be to God, the Lord of all created things." Such is the picture which is finally developed out of the simple Babylonian idea of the clear water which is enjoyed in Sheol by those who are perfectly pious. And countless millions of people at the present day are still dominated by these ideas of the torments of hell[1] and the bliss of Paradise.

As is well known, the idea that the deity employs messengers, angels — of whom the

[1] See Note, p. 119.

Egyptians are ignorant—is essentially Babylonian; and the conception of Cherubim and Seraphim, and of guardian angels attending upon man, is also to be traced back to Babylonia. A Babylonian ruler required an army of messengers to carry his commands into every land; so, too, the gods must have a legion of messengers or angels, always ready to do them service: messengers with the intelligence of men, and therefore of human form, yet withal provided with wings, to allow them to convey the commands of the deity through the air to the inhabitants of the earth.[1] These angel forms are likewise endowed with the piercing eye and the swift wings of the eagle; whilst those, moreover, whose principal duty was to guard the approach to the deity, were credited with having the unconquerable strength of the bull, or the fear-inspiring majesty of the lion, so that the angels of Babylonia and Assyria, like those in Ezekiel's vision, are very often represented as

[1] See Note, p. 120.

of hybrid form—as, for example, the winged bull-shaped Cherubim, with the contemplative face of a man (fig. 41). But we also meet with other representations of angels, such as that from the palace of Ashurnazirpal

Fig. 41.—Cherub.

Fig. 42.—Angel.

(fig. 42), which has the closest possible resemblance to our conception of angels. We shall always keep a warm place in our hearts for these noble and radiant figures which art has made so dear and so familiar to us. But demons and devils,[1] whether they

[1] See Note, p. 121.

hover before us as the enemies of man or as the earliest foes of God, should be banished for ever, once and for all, since we do not profess the dualism of ancient Persia. "He that maketh the light and createth darkness,

Fig. 43.—Combat between two demons.

Fig. 44.—A devil.

that maketh welfare and createth misfortune, I, Yahwè, am he that doeth all these things" —so does the greatest of the prophets of the Old Testament rightly teach (Is. xlv. 7). Let demons like those shewn here (fig. 43)—the picture is not without interest for the history of duelling—or distorted figures like the one in fig. 44, sink back for ever and for aye into the darkness of the Babylonian mounds out of which they arose.

And now to conclude. In the course of his excavations at Khorsabad, Victor Place discovered, among other things, the warehouses belonging to Sargon's palace: in one storeroom was earthenware of every size and shape, in another, iron utensils. Here, in the neatest order, lay large supplies of chains, nails, pegs, pickaxes, and mattocks, and the iron was so excellently worked, and so well preserved, that when struck it sounded like a bell—as a matter of fact, some of these articles, though five-and-twenty centuries old, could at once be made use of again by the Arab labourers.

That such productions of ancient Assyria should thus intrude themselves into our own time[1] in this impressive way strikes us, of course, as strange, and yet exactly the same has happened in the intellectual world. When we divide the Zodiac into twelve signs and

[1] See Note, p. 122.

style them the Ram, Bull, Twins, etc., when we divide the circle into 360 degrees, the hour into sixty minutes, and the minute into sixty seconds,—in all this the Sumerian-Babylonian culture is still living and operating even at the present day.

I may perhaps, then, have succeeded in shewing that many a Babylonian feature has attached itself even to our religious ideas through the medium of the Bible. When we have removed those conceptions, which, though derived, it is true, from highly-gifted peoples, are nevertheless purely human, and when we have freed our minds of firmly-rooted prejudice of every kind, religion itself, as extolled by the prophets and poets of the Old Testament, and as taught in its most sublime sense by Jesus, as also the religious feeling of our own hearts, is so little affected, that it may rather be said to emerge from the cleansing process in a truer and more sympathetic form. And at this point let me be allowed to add one last word on a subject which makes the Bible of such importance in the history of the world—its Monotheism. Here, too, Babel has quite recently opened up a new and unexpected prospect.

It is curious, but no one knows definitely what our word 'God' (*Gott*) originally means. Philologists hesitate between "awe-inspiring" and "that which exercises a spell." The word which the Semites, on the other hand, coined for God is clear. But it is more than this: it comprehends the idea of the deity in so full an extent, that by this one word alone is shattered the fable which tells us that "the Semites were at all times astonishingly lacking in religious instinct," and also the popular modern view which would see, both in the Yahwè-religion and in our Christian belief in God, something evolved out of such fetichism and animism as is characteristic of the South Sea cannibals or the Patagonians.

There is a beautiful passage in the Koran (vi. 75 *sqq.*), so beautiful that Goethe wished to see it treated dramatically. In it Mohammed imagines himself in Abraham's place and traces the probable workings of the patriarch's mind when arriving at the idea of Monotheism. He says: "When night had fallen and it was dark, Abraham went out into the darkness, and behold a star shone above him, then he cried joyfully, 'That is my Lord.' But when the star began to pale, he said, 'I like not them that become without lustre.' Then, when he saw the moon arise, shedding its light over the firmament, he cried overjoyed, 'That is my Lord.' But when the moon waned, he said, 'Alas, I needs must go astray.' Then in the morning, when the sun rose shining in splendour, he cried, 'This is my Lord, for he is indeed great!' But when the sun set, he said, 'O my people, I have nought to do with your worship of many gods, I turn my face to him who made heaven and earth.'"

The old Semitic word (if it may be called a word) for God, well known to us all from the words *Eli, Eli, lama azabtani* ("My God, my God, why hast thou forsaken me?"), is El,[1] and means the *Goal*—the Being to whom as to a goal the eyes of man looking heavenwards are

[1] See Note, p. 125.

turned, "on whom hangs the gaze of every man, to whom man looks out from afar" (Job xxxvi. 25), that Being towards whom man stretches forth his hands, after whom the human heart yearns away from the mutability and imperfection of earthly life—this Being the nomad Semitic tribes called El or God. And since the Divine Essence was viewed by them as a unity,[1] we find among the old North Semitic[2] tribes who settled in Babylonia about 2500 B.C., such personal names as "God has given," "God with me," "belonging to God," "God! turn again," "God is God," "if God be not my God," etc. But, further, through the kindness of the Head of the Department of Assyrian and Egyptian antiquities at the British Museum, I am able to give a representation of three small clay-tablets (figs. 45–47). What is there to be seen on these tablets? I shall be asked. Fragile, broken clay upon which are scratched characters scarcely legible! That is true, no doubt, yet they are precious for this reason: they can be dated

[1] See Note, p. 133. [2] See Note, p. 123.

with certainty, they belong to the age of Ḫammurabi, one in particular to the reign of his father Sin-mubaliṭ. But they are still more precious for another reason: they contain three names which, from the point of view

Figs. 45–47.—Three clay-tablets with the name of Yahwè.

of the history of religion, are of the most far-reaching importance:—

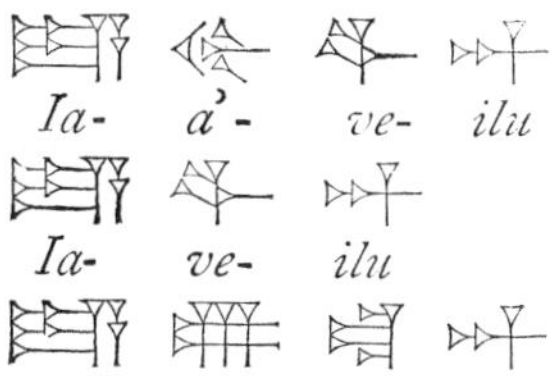

Ia- a'- ve- ilu

Ia- ve- ilu

Ia- ú- um- ilu

The names are ***Yahwè is God.*** Therefore Yahwè,[1] the Existing, the Enduring one (we

[1] See Note, p. 133.

have reasons for saying that the name may mean this), the one devoid of all change, not like us men, who to-morrow are but a thing of yesterday, but one who, above the starry vault which shines with everlasting regularity, lives and works from generation to generation—this 'Yahwè' was the spiritual possession of those same nomad tribes out of which after a thousand years the children of Israel were to emerge.

The religion of the immigrant Semites in Babylonia quickly succumbed[1] before the polytheism which for centuries had been current among the older, and oldest, dwellers in the land—a polytheism, however, from which, as far as its conception of the gods is concerned, our sympathy cannot altogether be withheld. For the gods of the Babylonians are living, omniscient, and omnipresent beings who hear the prayers of men, and, though they be angry with them for their sins, are yet ever ready to be conciliated and to take compassion. The representations, too, which are given of the

[1] See Note, p. 142.

deities in Babylonian art, as, for instance, that of the Sun-god of Sippar, sitting enthroned in his Holy of Holies (fig. 48; *cf.* also fig. 29), are far removed from all that is unlovely, ignoble, and grotesque.

The prophet Ezekiel (chap. i.) beholds God

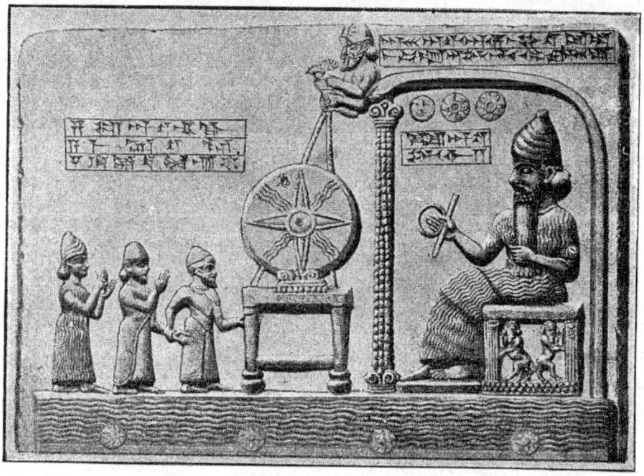

Fig. 48.—The Sun-god of Sippar.

driving in his living chariot formed of four winged beings, with the face of a man, a lion, an ox, and an eagle, and resting on the heads of the Cherubim (10) he sees a crystal surface (firmament), and upon this a throne as of sapphire, whereon God sits in human form, enveloped in a wondrous blaze of light. Now, a very old Babylonian cylinder seal (fig. 49) shows us a strikingly similar view of God: upon a wonderful ship, whose fore and aft parts taper off in the form of a sitting human

Fig. 49.—Cylinder-seal recalling Ezekiel's vision.

figure, two Cherubim are placed back to back, but with the face—which is of human form—turned towards us. Their position suggests that there are two others on the other side. On their backs rests a surface, and upon this is set a throne, whereon sits the deity, bearded and clad in a long mantle, with tiara upon his head, in the right hand, as it would seem, a sceptre and a ring. Behind the throne there stands an attendant of the god, at his beck and call, to be compared with "the man clothed in linen" (Ezek. ix. 3, x. 2), who, in like manner, executes the commands of Yahwè. In spite of all this, and notwithstanding that free and enlightened minds taught openly that Nergal and Nebo, Moon-god and Sun-god, the Thunder-god Ramman, and all other gods were one in Marduk, the god of light,[1] polytheism—gross polytheism—continued throughout three thousand years to be the Babylonian State religion, a solemn warning and example of the indolence of men and of peoples in religious matters, and of the immense power of an organised priesthood firmly founded upon it.

Even the Yahwè-faith, by which, as under a banner, Moses bound together in unity the twelve nomad tribes of Israel, was, and con-

[1] See Note, p. 143.

tinued to be, burdened with all kinds of human limitations: with those naïve anthropomorphic and anthropopathic views of the deity which are peculiar to the youth of the human race; with a heathen sacrificial cultus; with external forms of law, which did not prevent the people of pre-exilic times from continuous backsliding to the Baal and Astarte worship of the indigenous Canaanites, so that they even offered their sons and daughters as sacrifices to Baal; and, above all, with Israelite *exclusiveness*. Nor was that burden lifted until the prophets with admonitions—such as that of Joel, to rend the hearts and not the garments,—and the psalmists with utterances—such as, "The offerings that are pleasing to God are a contrite spirit and a broken heart" (Ps. li. 17)—urged *sincerity* in religion; until, with the preaching of Jesus, exhorting men to pray to God, the Father of us all, in spirit and in truth, a new era, that of the New Testament, dawned upon the world.

* * *

"Babel and the Bible."—What has been said represents but to a small extent the meaning of the excavations in Babylonia and Assyria for the history and progress of humanity. May it help to enforce recognition

Fig. 50.—The house of the German Expedition in Babylon.

of the fact that it was high time that Germany too should pitch her tent on the palm-crowned banks of the river of Paradise! Fig. 50 represents the dwelling of the Expedition sent out by the German Oriental Society. Out yonder on the ruins of Babylon, it is working ceaselessly, from morning till night, in heat and cold, for Germany's honour, and for Germany's learning.

We, too, "confess ourselves to be of the race which is struggling out of darkness into light." Sustained, like the archæological undertakings of the other nations, by the increasing interest of our people, and by the energetic support of our Government, ever animated anew by a feeling of gratitude for the gracious personal patronage which His Majesty the King and Emperor has been pleased to grant to it, and for the benevolent interest he has unceasingly taken in its efforts, the German Oriental Society, which was the last to appear on the field (only three years ago), will, assuredly, secure a place of honour under that sun which rises yonder in the East out of those mysterious hills.

Notes

LECTURE I

The Lecture published in the preceding pages was delivered for the German Oriental Society on the 13th of January 1902, in the Academy of Music at Berlin, in the presence of His Majesty the King and Emperor, and, at the most gracious wish of the Emperor, was repeated on the 1st of February in the Royal Palace at Berlin.

The meaning of the title has, with few exceptions, been quite correctly understood: "Babel as the interpreter and illustrator of the Bible." So the *Schlesische Zeitung* for 24th January 1902: "Babel and Bible—this was the short but comprehensive heading, signifying that the speaker intended to discuss the results of the excavations in Babylonia and Assyria in their bearing on the Bible."

Out of the multitude of rejoinders and more detailed reviews that have been called forth by "Babel and Bible"—in so far as they have come to my knowledge since my return from Babylonia, and have proved to be of interest, scientifically or otherwise—attention may be specially called to the following. My own notes, which I have added, are only meant to serve a passing purpose. Not until the lectures on "Babel and the Bible" have been continued and concluded will the time be ripe for a complete critical review of the replies they have called forth.

I.

J. BARTH, *Babel und israelitisches Religionswesen.* A Lecture. Berlin, 1902; 36 pp.

Prof. Dr. KARL BUDDE, *Das Alte Testament und die Ausgrabungen.* Giessen, 1903. (A Lecture, delivered May 29, 1902, at the Theological Conference at Giessen); 39 pages, of which, however, only pp. 1–10 concern "Babel und Bibel."

The following passage in Budde's lecture may be fixed upon here, on account of its bearings (p. 6 *sq.*): "At all events, the calm decisiveness with which he emphasises certain truths, which have long ago been accepted as everyday truths, but which are often still condemned in the leading ecclesiastical circles as dreadful heresies, is deserving of our gratitude. For example, the compilation of the Pentateuch from a series of 'very different sources,' the dependence upon Babylonian myths of large portions of the primæval history as given in the Bible—the creation, the flood, the Sethite genealogy—the futility of all attempts to bring the biblical account of the creation into harmony with the results of Natural Science."

Dr. Johannes Döller, Imperial and Royal Court Chaplain and Director of Studies at the Frintaneum, Vienna, *Bibel und Babel oder Babel und Bibel? Eine Entgegnung auf Prof. F. Delitzsch' "Babel und Bibel."* Paderborn, 1903.

Prof. Dr. HOMMEL, *Die altorientalischen Denkmäler und das Alte Testament. Eine Erwiderung auf Prof. Fr. Delitzsch's "Babel und Bibel."* Berlin, 1902; 38 pp.

"Decidedly the simplest and most convenient course to take now would be to hold oneself aloof from the whole theory of separate sources. This, however, will not do on account of the various duplicate accounts which, however much one might wish it, are not to be explained away, and which we can observe with special clearness, particularly in the biblical accounts of the creation and deluge" (p. 15).—"It can easily be shewn that the whole account of the creation (Gen. i.–ii. 4.) is in the closest touch with a Chaldæan account of the creation *which is no longer ex-*

tant" (p. 18).—"The word *šapattu* for Sabbath is seen at the first glance to be a word in Babylonian borrowed from the Chaldæan; if genuinely Babylonian, it must have been *šabtu* (from *wašab*, 'to sit, rest')" (p. 18 *sq.*).

Dr. Alfred Jeremias, pastor of the Lutheran Church at Leipzig, *Im Kampfe um Babel und Bibel. Ein Wort zur Verständigung und Abwehr.* Third, enlarged edition. Leipzig, 1903; 45 pp.

Prof. D. R. Kittel, *Die babylonischen Ausgrabungen und die biblische Urgeschichte.* Second, unaltered edition. Leipzig, 1902; 36 pp. See also under Section II., page 91.

W. Knieschke, pastor at Sieversdorf, *Bibel und Babel, El und Bel. Eine Replik auf Friedrich Delitzschs Babel und Bibel.* Westend-Berlin, 1902; 64 pp.

Prof. Dr. phil. und theol. Eduard König, *Bibel und Babel. Eine kulturgeschichtliche*

Skizze. Sixth, enlarged edition, with reference to the most recent literature on the subject of Babel and Bible. Berlin, 1902; 60 pp.

The verdict of P. Keil (*cf.* p. 90 below) is as follows: "In general it would appear from König's pamphlet that he is not too much at home in Assyriology. His treatment of *Yahve-ilu* is but calculated to strengthen this impression. Why venture on the slippery ice of Assyriology?" (*op. cit.*, p. 6). As a matter of fact, hardly anything more mediocre could be imagined than pp. 8–10, 38 *sqq.*, 45–49 of König's essay. God "is the spiritual reality existing before the world and outliving all its phases, the heart of the world which throbs throughout the world and remains true in all the changes of history" (p. 53). "Harmony between God and man forms the glowing gate of the dawn of God's path in history, and harmony between God and man is the flag-decked haven through which God's path in history flows into eternity" (p. 54). "In Babel men strove to attain heaven, in the Bible heaven descends into the wretched life of man" (p. 59). What a fine resounding tone it all has! And yet it cannot blind us to the fact that even König denies the verbal inspiration of the Old Testament, accuses the Old Testament of "undeniable errors" (p. 14), and thus strips it of its character of divine revelation, as understood by the Church. A ravening wolf in spite of his sheep's clothing. Note also the review by H. Winckler in the supplement to the *Nord-deutsche Allgemeine Zeitung*, Sunday, August 3, 1902.—König's pamphlet has now appeared in a seventh, enlarged edition, "with a criticism of Delitzsch's latest utterances on Babel and Bible."

Prof. D. SAM. OETTLI, *Der Kampf um Bibel und Babel. Ein religionsgeschichtlicher Vortrag*. Second edition. Leipzig, 1902; 32 pp.

My citations are from the first edition. Oettli, too, observes (p. 13) that "according to the almost universally prevailing conviction, the existing state of the text compels us to abandon the overstrained dogma of inspiration, which sees in Holy Writ the unerring word of God, inspired even down to its very wording." Oettli's protest against the assumption of an original revelation is very significant and acceptable (pp. 12–15); note, in particular, p. 14: "That tradition of a concrete knowledge of the world based upon original revelation, whose form in Israel is pure, but everywhere else degenerate, is a *pure hypothesis*, for which no valid historical proof can be produced. It is, therefore, all the more perverse to wish to stamp acceptance of it as the mark of an unbroken belief in Scripture. It derives its sole strength from the dogma of inspiration, which, although already abandoned, still influences us in a decisive manner from out the dark background of our consciousness. In many cases, indeed, it is born of an interest in the faith that claims our respect, but not of any indisputable historical attestation."

Rabb. Dr. LUDW. A. ROSENTHAL, *Babel und Bibel oder Babel gegen Bibel? Ein Wort zur Klärung.* Berlin, 1902; 31 pp.

Cf. P. Keil (p. 6 note): "Rosenthal indulges in elaborations as to principles; but his object is not quite clear."

II.

Prof. BRUNO BAENTSCH, Jena, *Babel und Bibel. Eine Prüfung des unter diesem Titel erschienenen Vortrages von Friedrich Delitzsch besonders auf die darin enthaltenen religionsgeschichtlichen Ausführungen,* in the Protestantische Monatshefte, edited by D. Julius Websky. VI., Heft 8 (August 15, 1902). Berlin, 1902. *Cf.* also two articles, signed B. B., "*Noch einmal Babel und Bibel,*" in the Thüringe Rundschau of the 2nd and 9th of March 1902.

Prof. D. C. H. CORNILL, Breslau, *Deutsche Litteraturzeitung*, 1902, No. 27 (July 5).

HEINRICH DANNEIL (Schönebeck a. E.), *Babel und Bibel:* Magdeburgische Zeitung, No. 25, 1902, Beiblatt.

Privatdocent Dr. W. ENGELKEMPER, Münster, *Babel und Bibel:* Wissenschaftliche Beilage zur Germania, 1902, Nos. 31 (July 31) and 32 (August 7). Berlin, 1902.

Influenced by König and Jensen. The following words of this Catholic theologian may be cited for a specific reason: "Although Christianity is founded upon the writings and tradition of the New Testament, the truth of the New Testament is nevertheless most intimately connected with that of the Old, and is historically and logically a consequence of the Old."

Prof. D. GUNKEL, *Babylonische und biblische Urgeschichte.* Christliche Welt, XVII., 1903, No. 6 (Feb. 5), cols. 121–134.

Prof. Dr. PETER JENSEN, *Babel und Bibel:* Die christliche Welt, XVI., 1902, No. 21 (May 22), cols. 487–494.

Jensen's criticism proves to be sound in no

single point, and will, therefore, do no lasting harm to the cause of truth.

Franz Kaulen, Bonn, *Babel und Bibel:* Literarischer Handweiser zunächst für alle Katholiken deutscher Zunge. XL., Nos. 766 and 767, 1901–2.

The notice concludes as follows: "The results of the three years' work of the German Expedition do not as yet come up to our expectations, especially as compared with the results obtained by the American Expedition in the same time. The share which the German people have had in it does not make up for the deep-rooted harm involved in the tendency of German research to set Science, in this case 'Babylonology,' in the place of Divine Revelation. Through Delitzsch, Babel's ineradicable characteristic, that of being the opponent of God and of Divine Revelation, has been destined to be transferred to this record and to the German Oriental Society." *I protest indignantly against this latter aspersion.*

The German Oriental Society has nothing whatever to do with the views represented in my lectures on "Babel and the Bible"; indeed, both the Society and myself would be sincerely grateful if other scholars, and above all Franz Kaulen himself, could find the time and inclination to instruct the members of the German Oriental Society on the questions mooted by me, or on kindred ones.

P. KEIL, London, *Babel und Bibel.* Pastor bonus. Zeitschrift für kirchliche Wissenschaft und Praxis, edited by Domkapitular Dr. P. Einig. XV., parts 1, 2, 3 (Oct. 1, Nov. 1, Dec. 1, 1902).

"The uninitiated person has not the faintest idea of the difficulty in interpreting inscriptions. In contrast to the 37 Hebrew characters, there are no less than some 20,000 groups of signs and about 600 individual signs. It is, therefore, self-evident what opportunity there is for error in the course of decipherment" (p. 6, with note). Apart from this distorted statement, this criticism, by a Catholic priest, evidences a laudable knowledge of Assyriology with which nothing I have met with in the case of evangelical theologians, Pastor A. Jeremias excepted, can be compared.

Prof. D. R. KITTEL, Leipzig, *Jahve in "Babel und Bibel":* Theologisches Literaturblatt, XXIII., No. 17 (April 25, 1902).

Contains a number of errors, among them being the statement that in the three names *Ia've-ilu, Iave-ilu, Iaum-ilu,* it is a question of one and the same person. Also, *Noch einmal Jahve in "Babel und Bibel": op. cit.,* No. 18 (May 2, 1902). Also, *Der Monotheismus in "Babel und Bibel,"* Allegemeine evangelisch-lutherische Kirchenzeitung, 1902, No. 17 (April 25, 1902).

Distrikts-Rabbiner Dr. S. MEYER, Regensburg, *Die Hypothesen-gläubigen:* Deutsche Israelitische Zeitung, XIX., No. 8 (20th February 1902); and *Nochmals Babel und Bibel, op. cit.,* No. 10 (6th March).

Babel und Bibel: Neue Preussische (Kreuz-) Zeitung, 1902, No. 211 (7th May). Signed ——l [Lic. theol. Prof. Riedel, Greifswald].

WOLFF, *Babel und Bibel:* Evangelische Kirchenzeitung, 1902, No. 28 (cols. 657–662).

P. 7. MURASHÛ & SONS. *Vide The Babylonian Expedition of the University of Pennsylvania.* Series A, Cuneiform Texts. Vol. IX. Business Documents of Murashû & Sons of Nippur, dated in the reign of Artaxerxes I. (464–424 B.C.), by H. V. Hilprecht and A. T. Clay, Ph.D. Philadelphia, 1898.

P. 14. "And as his father's brother took no care for his widowed mother."

The cuneiform words in question cannot indeed be interpreted with certainty, but the mention of the father's brother in immediate connection with the information that the child had never known its father, that the latter, therefore, had died before its birth, leads me to suppose that according to Babylonian custom the brother-in-law of the wife, "the father's brother," had duties towards the wife assigned to him, of a nature somewhat similar to those of the Israelitish גֹּאֵל.

P. 16. The types are taken from the work by Henry George Tomkins, *Studies on the Times of Abraham.* London. Plate V., "Eight typical plates in profile drawn by the author."

P. 27. PROCESSIONS OF THE GODS.—We read in Isaiah xlv. 20: "They have no knowledge that carry their graven image of wood, and pray unto a God that cannot help," and in xlvi. 1: "Bel has sunk down, Nebo is bowed down, their idols are fallen to the lot of the beasts and to the cattle, the things (*i.e.* fabrications) that ye carried about are made a load, a burden to the weary beasts." There can be but few commentators here who do not think in connection with these passages of the Babylonian processions of the gods, in which Bel and Nebo were carried in ceremonious progress through the streets of Babel.—

According to Jensen (*op. cit.*, col. 488) I am 'incorrect' in finding a mention of processions of gods in Isaiah xlvi. 1.

P. 33. AARON'S BLESSING (Num. vi. 24 *sqq.*).—What I have said as to the meaning of the phrase in the blessing of Aaron, "Yahwè lift up his face to thee," *i.q.*, "turn his favour, his love, towards thee," holds good in every respect. When spoken of men, "to lift the countenance to anyone or to anything" means nothing more than "to look up at" (so 2 Ki. ix. 32). It is used in Job xxii. 26 (*cf.* xi. 15), as well as in 2 Sam. ii. 22, with reference to a man who, free from guilt and fault, can look up at God or at his fellow-men. This meaning, of course, is not appropriate if the words are spoken of God. Then it must mean precisely the same thing as the Assyrian, "to raise the eyes to anyone," that is to say, to find pleasure in one, to direct one's love towards him; therefore not quite the same as to take heed of one (as in Siegfried-Stade's *Hebräisches Wörterbuch*, p. 441). If it were so, "the Lord lift up his countenance to thee" would be equivalent to "the Lord keep thee." When Jensen (*op. cit.*, col. 491) lays stress on the fact that the Assyrian expression is literally, not to lift up "the face," but to lift up "the eyes," he might with equal justice deny that Assyrian *bît Ammân* means the same thing as the Hebrew *b*^{e}*nê Ammôn*. As a matter of fact, whereas the prevailing Hebrew usage is "if it be right in thine eyes," the Assyrian says in every case, "if it be right in thy countenance" (*ina pânika; cf. šumma* [*ina*] *pân šarri maḫir*); "eyes" and "countenance" interchange in such phrases as this. In Hebrew we find "to lift up the eyes to one" used as equivalent to "to conceive an affection for one," only with reference to human, sensual love (Gen. xxxix. 7). The value of the Assyrian phrase, "to lift up the eyes to any one," in its bearing on the Aaronite blessing, rests in the fact that it is used with especial predilection (though not exclusively, as Jensen imagines) of the gods who direct their love towards a chosen individual or some privileged state. When Jensen concludes (col. 490) that my choice of this example as a specimen of the advantages to be obtained from Assyrian linguistic analogies is "a failure," I gladly console myself with the reflection that this fact of a deeper meaning in the blessing of Aaron, which we owe to cuneiform literature, obtained many years ago the assent of no less a person than Franz Delitzsch.

P. 34. Note the date 2250 B.C., not 1050, as was given by a number of journals, following a printer's error in the *Berliner Tageblatt*. When on page 34 *et seq.*, speaking of Ḫammurabi, I said, "He prepared a great code, which defined the civil law in all its branches," this was at the time a mere inference, chiefly based upon a number of tablets from the library of Ashurbanipal. This code of law has now actually been found engraved on a block of diorite, nearly 8 feet high, containing, apart from the prologue and epilogue, 282 paragraphs of laws. This unique discovery was made by the French archæologist de Morgan and V. Scheil on the Acropolis of Susa in December–January 1901–02. *Cf.* Lecture II.

P. 39. Canaan at the time of the Israelite Incursion, a "domain completely pervaded by Babylonian culture." This fact, which J. Barth attacks on trivial grounds, obtains ever wider recognition. *Cf.* Alfred Jeremias in the "Zeitgeist" of the *Berliner Tageblatt* of 16th February 1903: "Further, at the time of the immigration of the 'children of Israel,' Canaan was subject to the especial influence of Babylonian civilization. About 1450 the Canaanites, like all the peoples of the Nearer East, wrote in the Babylonian cuneiform character, and in the Babylonian language. This fact, proved by the literature of the time, forces us to assume that the influence of Babylonian thought had been exerted for centuries previously. Of late Canaan itself seems to wish to bear witness. The excavation of an ancient Canaanite castle by Prof. Sellin has brought to light an altar with Babylonian genii and trees of life, and Babylonian seals."

It may be briefly recalled here that the religion of the Canaanites with their god Tammuz, and their Asherahs, bears unmistakable marks of Babylonian influence, and that before the immigration of the children of Israel a place in the neighbourhood of Jerusalem was called *Bît-Ninib*, after the Babylonian god Ninib. There may have been actually in Jerusalem itself a *bît Ninib*, a temple of the god Ninib. See *Keilinschriftliche Bibliothek*, V., No. 183, 15, and *cf.* Zimmern, in the third edition of Schrader's *Die Keilinschriften und das Alte Testament*, second half, p. 411. *Cf.* also Lecture II., p. 184.

P. 40. The Sabbath.—The vocabulary II. R. 32, No. 1, mentions, among divers kinds of 'days,' a *ûm nûḫ libbi* (l. 16, *a*, *b*), that is to say, a day for the quieting of the heart (*sc.*, of the gods), with its synonym *ša-pat-tum*. This word, in view of the frequent use of the sign *pat* for *bát* (*e.g.*, *šú-pat*, var. *bat*, 'dwelling'; Tig. vi. 94), might, and in view of the syllabary 82, 9–18, 4159, col. 1, 24, where *UD* (Sumer. *ú*) is rendered by *ša-bat-tum*, must be understood as *šabattum.* The statement in the latter syllabary not only at the same time confirms the view that the word *šabattum* means a *day*, but it may also explain the *šabattum* to be *the* day κατ' ἐξοχήν (because the day of the gods?). Again, neither from 83, 1–8, 1330, col. 1, 25, where ***ZUR*** is rendered by *ša-bat-tim* (following immediately upon *nuḫḫu*), nor from IV. 8, where **TE** is rendered by *ša-bat-tim* [why not, as elsewhere, in the nominative?], may it be inferred with any degree of certainty that *šabattu* could mean "appeasement (of the gods), expiation, penitential prayer" (so Jensen in ***Z. A.*** iv., 1889, pp. 274 *sqq.*), or that the verb *šabâtu* could mean "to conciliate" or "to be conciliated" (Jensen in *Christliche Welt*, col. 492)—the latter all the less since the verb *šabâtu* is hitherto only attested as a synonym of *gamâru* (V. R. 28, 14, *e*, *f*). For *šabattu*, therefore, the only meaning that may be justifiably assumed at present is "ending (of work), cessation, keeping holiday (from work)." It seems to me that the compiler of the syllabary 83, 1–8, 1330, arrived at ***ZUR*** and ***TE*** = *šabbatim* from the equations ***UD. ZUR*** and ***UD. TE*** = *ûm nuḫḫi* or *puššuḫi* = *ûm šabattim*.

The Babylonian *šabattu* is accordingly *the day of the quieting* of the heart of the gods and *the day of the resting* from man's work (as will be readily understood, the latter is essential to the former). When, therefore, in the well-known calendar of festivals, IV. R. 32, 33, the seventh, fourteenth, twenty-first, and twenty-eighth days of a month are expressly characterized as days whereon every kind of business should rest—should we not see in these days no other than the *šabattu*-day? The words in question in the calendar of festivals may, according to our present knowledge, be rendered thus: "The shepherd of the great peoples shall not eat roasted or smoked (?) flesh (var. anything touched by fire), shall not change his garment, shall not put on white raiment, shall not offer a sacrifice [are these the prohibitions of universal application, even as regards the flocks of the shepherd? the particular prohibitions follow]; the King shall not mount his chariot, as ruler he shall pronounce no judgment; the Magus shall not give oracles in a secret place (one removed from profane approach), the physician shall not lay his hand on the sick —*it [the day] is not appropriate for any business whatever* (? *ana kal ṣibûti*; *ṣibûtu* here, it would seem, used like צְבוּ, *ṣ*ᵉ*bū*, in Dan. vi. 18: "business, matter"). Accordingly it remains true that the Hebrew Sabbath, "in the last resort," originates in a Babylonian institution. No more than this was maintained. When, therefore, König emphasises that the Israelite Sabbath received its specific sanction on account of its tending to "the exercise of humanity towards those who serve, and towards the brute creation," there is no occasion for us to dispute with him on the subject. The setting apart of the seventh day in particular to be the day in which we are to refrain from business of every kind explains itself, as I shewed years ago, from the fact that the number seven seemed to the Babylonians, as to others, to be an 'evil' number (whence their description of the seventh, fourteenth, twenty-first, twenty-eighth days in the above-mentioned calendar as ***UD. ḪUL. GÀL.***, *i.e.*, evil days). Alfred Jeremias (*op. cit.*, p. 25) aptly recalls the Talmudic story, according to which Moses arranged with Pharaoh a day of rest for his people, and when asked which he thought the most suitable for the purpose, answered: "The seventh, which is dedicated to the Planet Saturn; works done on this day do not, as a rule, prosper, in any case."

P. 45. THE DELUGE.—Oettli says (p. 20 *sq.*): "The Old Testament traditional materials are steeped in an atmosphere of ethical monotheism, and by this bath are cleansed from the elements that are confused and confusing, whether from the point of view of religion or of ethics. The flood is no longer the operation of the blind anger of the gods, but a punishment of a depraved race by the just God, moved by moral considerations." This is not correct. It was already to be inferred from the account of Berossus that in the case of the Babylonians, also, the deluge was a punishment (*Sündflut*); note his words: "the rest cried aloud, when a voice commanded them to be *God-fearing*, since Xisuthros, *on account of his piety*, was removed to be with the Gods." If it may be inferred from this that the Babylonian Noah escaped the judgment of the flood merely on account of his piety, while the rest of mankind was destroyed on account of their increasing sinfulness, the inference is confirmed in the cuneiform account in the words which Ea addresses after the deluge to Bel, who had brought it about: "upon the sinner lay his sins," etc.—König (p. 32) observes: "The spirit of the two traditions is totally different. One feature shews this at once: the Babylonian hero saves his belongings, dead and alive, but in the two Biblical accounts we have in its place the higher point of view, the preservation of the brute creation." What blind infatuation! Even Xisuthros, according to the fragments of Berossus, received the command "to take in winged and four-footed beasts," and the original cuneiform account expressly says, "I embarked on the ship the cattle of the field, the wild beasts of the field." Accordingly, König himself must recognise the "higher point of view" in the Babylonian story as well.

P. 50. The Creation.—For the Babylonian story of creation, see L. W. King, *The Seven Tablets of Creation, or the Babylonian and Assyrian Legends concerning the Creation of the World and of Mankind.* Vol. I. *English translations.* London, 1902. "Mythological features" (p. 50, ll. 15 *sqq.*) within the Biblical account of the creation. As to the assumption of the existence of a state of chaos, Oettli very truly remarks (p. 12): "The conception of original matter, which was not derived from God's creative action, but has rather to be overcome by it, cannot have grown up upon the mother-soil of Israel's religion, which, at any rate at the high level reached by the prophets, looks at things from a strictly monotheistic standpoint, and therefore excludes the dualistic conflict of two opposing primæval principles." Wellhausen's remark may also be recalled here: "But chaos being granted, all the rest is spun out of it; all that follows is reflexion, systematic construction, which we can easily control from point to point." Traces of polytheistic traits, also, adhere to the Elohistic story of the creation. In Gen. i. 26 we read, "let *us* make men in *our* image, according to *our* likeness," where the assumption of a so-called *pluralis majestaticus* is, to judge by Hebrew usage elsewhere, certainly not excluded (*cf.* Isaiah xlvi. 5), but rather far-fetched. (Observe the words of Yahwè in iii. 22, "See! the man has become as *one of us*.") On this Oettli rightly remarks (p. 10): "It is not easy to bring the use of the plural in a soliloquy, before man had been created, into agreement with the strict monotheism of a later date; nor is the divine likeness in which man is framed easily reconciled with that spirituality of Yahwè, which is so strongly emphasised at a later date; when we, renouncing all exegetical devices, allow the words to bear their simple and most obvious meaning; even though we admit that the Biblical writer has given a higher meaning to these originally foreign elements in accordance with his religious attitude." In fact, Gen. i. 26 and Isaiah xlvi. 5 are irreconcilable contradictions. The polytheistic colouring, distinguishing gods and goddesses, is peculiarly striking in Gen. i. 27, when the three members of the verse are considered in close connection one with the other; "and God created man in his image, in the image of God created he him, *male and female* created he them." But this cannot be regarded as certain.

P. 56.—Oettli, also (p. 11), following Gunkel (*Schöpfung und Chaos*, pp. 29–114), comes to a conclusion identical with that on p. 56: "There are enough allusions in the prophetical and poetical literature of the

Old Testament to make it palpably clear that the old [Babylonian] creation-myth survived —and in a highly-coloured form—in the popular conceptions of Israel." And again, "There are in fact cases enough where the original mythical signification of the monsters *tehôm, livyāthân, tannîn, râhâb,* is unmistakably evident." Oettli cites Job ix. 13 and Is. li. 9 (where, moreover, 'pierced' might be better than 'dishonoured'). In fact, when Is. li. 10 proceeds with the words, "Art thou not it that dried up the sea, the water of the great Tehôm, that made the depths of the sea a way for the ransomed to pass over?" the prophet actually couples "those mythical reminiscences" with the deliverance from Egypt, Yahwè's second famous exploit on the waters of Tehôm. And it cannot occur to any one who recalls how Yahwè's great achievement, when the children of Israel crossed the Red Sea, is elsewhere described and extolled (*e.g.*, Ps. cvi. 9–11, lxxviii. 13), to apply to any but primæval times the words in Ps.

lxxiv. 13 *sq.*: "Thou brakest the heads of the dragons in the waters, thou didst dash to pieces the heads of the sea-monsters (*livyāthân*)." *Livyāthân*, according to Job iii. 8 also, is the personification of the dark chaotic primæval flood, the sworn foe of the light.

If König himself is unwillingly obliged to admit (p. 27) that the book of Job, in ix. 13 ("God turns not his anger, the helpers of *râhâb* brake in pieces under him"), and in xxvi. 12 ("in his power he smote the sea and in his wisdom he dashed *râhâb* to pieces"), "alludes, in all probability, to the subjection of the primæval ocean," Jensen would certainly seem to stand quite alone when he asserts (*op. cit.*, col. 490), "where the Old Testament speaks of a struggle on the part of Yahwè against serpents and crocodile-like creatures, there is no occasion to assume with Delitzsch and with a considerable number of other Assyriologists [add: as also with Gunkel and most Old Testament theologians] a connection with the Babylonian myth of a Tiâmat-struggle."

P. 52.—Oettli, also, very truly avows (p. 17) that "all subordination of the researches of Natural Science to the Biblical representation is wholly perverse, and is the more unintelligible as the external details in the second account of the creation and in many other passages in the Old Testament are conceived in a manner quite unlike the first. Let us, therefore, unreservedly leave to Science that which belongs to it." When, however, he proceeds: "But let us also give to God that which is God's; the world is a creation of God's almighty will, which continuously pervades it as its living law—this the first page of Genesis tells us," it is less possible to concur. Faith claims, and many passages in the Old Testament assert, that God is the Almighty Creator of heaven and earth, but it is just the first page of Genesis that does not ("in the beginning God created the heaven and the earth—and the earth was waste and desolate," etc.); it leaves unanswered the question, "Whence did chaos originate?" Besides, even among the Babylonians the creation of the heavens and of the earth is ascribed to the gods, and the life of all animate creatures is regarded as resting in their hands.

To FIGURES 37 ('the god Marduk') on p. 51, and 38 ('the conflict with the dragon') on p. 52, Jensen (*op cit.*, col. 489) observes with reference to Tiâmat: "Berossus calls this creature a woman, she is the mother of the gods, has a husband and a lover, and nowhere throughout Assyrian or Babylonian literature is there to be found even the slightest hint that this creature is regarded otherwise than as a woman without any limitation." Nothing can be more perverse than this assertion, which contradicts not merely what I have said, but also a fact recognised by all Assyriologists. Or is it no longer true that as a woman gives birth to human beings, and young lions are brought forth by lionesses, that, therefore, a creature which gives birth to (*ittalad*, see Creation-epic, III. 24, and often), *ṣirmaḫḫê*, *i.e.*, gigantic serpents, must itself be a great, powerful serpent, a *δράκων μέγας* or some serpent-like monster? And, as a matter of fact, is not Tiâmat represented in Babylonian art as a great serpent (see, for example, Cheyne's English translation of the Book of the Prophet Isaiah in Haupt's edition of the Bible, p. 206)? Nor do I by any means see in the scene represented in fig. 38 a perfectly exact portrayal of Marduk's conflict with the Dragon, as described to us in the creation-epic; on the contrary, I speak expressly and cautiously of a conflict between "the power of light and the power of darkness" in general. It can be realised at once that in the representation of this conflict, especially in that of the monster Tiâmat, there was wide scope for the imagination. A dragon could be represented in the most manifold way, such as we see in fig. 38, or on a stone found in Babylon (see fig. 51), or in the form of the *ṣirruššû* (or *mušruššû*), which, indeed, appears in the Epic as only one of the eleven monsters called into life by Tiâmat, but which, according to II. R. 19, 17 *b*, can, and in Babylonian art actually does, represent Tiâmat herself. For the beast which is placed at the feet of the god Marduk in fig. 37, and was declared by me to be a representation of the

Fig. 51.—Marduk's conflict with the dragon.

dragon Tiâmat, has since been clearly proved to be such by the German excavations. The representations of the *ṣirruššû* found on the Gate of Ishtar at Babylon in relief, unmistakably correspond to the animal figure familiar to us from our illustration (fig. 37). If, in addition to what has been said here, reference is made further to Zimmern's exposition in the third edition of Schrader's *Die Keilinschriften und das Alte Testament*, 2nd half, pp. 502 *ff.*, the conclusion will undoubtedly be reached that Jensen's polemic against "Babel und Bibel" in the *Christliche Welt*, col. 489 *sq.*, is entirely unjustified.

To Page 54. My words are by no means intended to suggest that "even the fundamental laws of the human instinct of self-preservation and morality, such as love for one's neighbour, betray Babylonian origin" (as was to be read in a number of newspapers, following the *Berliner Tageblatt*). When a Babylonian priest asks (IV. R. 51, 50–53 *a*): "Has he broken into the house of his neighbour? Has he approached the wife of his neighbour? Has he shed the blood of his neighbour? Has he taken to himself the garment of his neighbour?" I conclude, as I have unambiguously said on p. 53, simply this, that prohibitions such as these are indelibly stamped on "every human heart."

The following statement of P. Keil (*op. cit.*, p. 3 *sq.*) is therefore absolutely incorrect: "Even the moral law, the conception of sin . . . . originate from Babylon. Delitzsch, it is true, does not say it so bluntly, but his exposition leads us to suppose that in these matters he admits connections between Babel and the Bible other than those which are purely collateral."

P. 56. THE FALL.—Anyone who reads my remarks on p. 55 without bias must admit that in dealing with the representation of a Babylonian seal (fig. 39), reproduced on p. 56, on the one hand, and with the Biblical story of the Fall, on the other, my only aim was to emphasise the circumstance that *the serpent as the corrupter of the woman* is a significant feature common to both. The fact that the two Babylonian figures are clothed, naturally prevented me, also, from regarding the tree as the tree "of knowledge of good and evil." It seems to me at least more probable that there may be traced in the biblical narrative in Gen. chap. ii. *sq.*, another and older form which recognized but one tree in the middle of the garden—the Tree of Life. Note how in ii. 9 the words, "and the tree of the knowledge of good and evil," seem to be tacked on, as it were, and how the narrator, busied with the newly introduced tree of knowledge, so entirely forgets the tree of life (see iii. 3), that in ii. 16 he—quite inadvertently—actually makes God allow man to eat of the tree of life (in contradiction with iii. 22). In regard to the tree, and that alone, I agree with the late C. P. Tiele when he sees in the Babylonian representation, "a god with his male or female worshippers partaking of the fruit of the tree of life," "a picture of the hope of immortality," as also with Hommel, who observes (p. 23): "the most important point is that it is quite evident that the tree was originally thought of as a conifer—a pine or cedar—whose fruit increased the power of life and of procreation; there is, accordingly, an unmistakable allusion to the holy cedar of Eridu, the typical tree of Paradise in the Chaldæan and Babylonian legends." Jensen, also, (col. 488) decides as follows: "If the representation has any reference to the story of the Fall, it might most preferably represent a scene in which a god forbids the first-created woman to partake of the fruit of the tree of life." That one of the figures is distinguished by horns, the usual symbol of strength and conquest (see Amos vi. 13) in Babylonia as also in Israel, is, I take it, a very fine touch on the part of the artist, indicating unmistakably the different sexes of the two clothed human figures; and whoever prefers to see in the serpent behind the woman a "crooked stroke," "an ornamental dividing line," may do so—few will agree with him.

Many scholars are of the same opinion as myself. So Hommel, for instance (p. 23): "the woman and the writhing serpent behind her express themselves clearly enough"; and Jensen (col. 488): "a serpent stands or crawls behind the woman." As to the nature of this serpent, nothing definite can be said so long as we are dependent upon this pictorial representation alone. One is most disposed to regard it as one of the forms of Tiâmat, who—like Leviathan in Job iii. 8, and "the old serpent" in the Apocalypse—would thus be assumed to be still in existence. But this is very uncertain, and I have therefore borne in mind II. R. 51, 44, where, doubtless following some as yet unknown myth, a Babylonian canal is named after "the Serpent-god who shatters (destroys) the dwelling of life." This passage seems to me to argue at once against Jensen's view, that we may perhaps see in the two figures, two gods that dwell by the tree of life, and in the serpent, its guardian. Moreover, Zimmern (*Die Keilinschriften und das Alte Testament*, 3rd ed., second half, p. 504 *sq.*) takes the serpent-god to be "without doubt ultimately identical with the chaos-monster." It may be noted, in passing, that the text D. T. 67, published in Haupt's *Akkadische und sumerische Keilschrifttexte*, p. 119, may deserve consideration in the future for its bearing upon the biblical narrative of the Fall. It is a bilingual text which tells of a virgin, the "mother of sin," who, having committed an offence for which she is severely punished, bursts into bitter tears—"carnal intercourse hath she come to know, kisses hath she come to know"—and whom we find later on lying in the dust smitten by the fatal glance of the deity.

P. 59. "May his name continue to be blessed," etc.

In the code of Ḫammurabi (xxvii. 34 *et seq.*), we find the sinner cursed with the words: "May God forcibly extinguish him from among the living upon earth, and debar his departed spirit upon earth from fresh water in Hades."

The last passage also confirms the great antiquity of the Babylonian conception of the condition of the pious after death.

P. 59. The passage in Job xxiv. 18 *sq.* is to be found translated and explained in a satisfactory philological manner in my *Das Buch Iob* (Leipzig, 1902): "cursed be their portion upon earth. He turneth not by the way of the vineyards, the wilderness and also the heat shall despoil them, they go astray imploring snow-water. Compassion forgetteth him, the worm sucks at him, he shall be no more remembered," etc. The passage, thus rightly conceived, forms the welcome bridge to the New Testament image of the pit (Hell), glowing with heat, waterless, and full of torments, and of the garden which the Oriental mind cannot conceive of as lacking water, an abundant flow of running water. When Cornill (*op. cit.*, col. 1683) remarks: "I believe I also am tolerably acquainted with the Book of Job . . . . but there is absolutely nothing of the sort in Job xxiv. 18 *sq.*," such words only strengthen the pleasant feeling that the philological comprehension of the Old Testament no longer necessarily permeates the commentaries of the Old Testament theologians.

P. 62. The concluding verse of the book of the prophet Isaiah (ch. lxvi. 24: "and they shall go forth and look with joy upon the dead bodies of those that have revolted from me: how their worm dieth not, neither is their fire quenched: and they are an abomination to all flesh") implies that those whose bodies are buried in the earth will be everlastingly gnawed by worms, and those whose bodies are burnt with fire shall suffer this death by fire continuously. The passage is important in two respects: in the first place, it shows that cremation is thought of as standing entirely on the same level with inhumation, and that, accordingly, there is not the slightest opposition to cremation from the Biblical side; in the second place, it follows that the words, "where their worm dieth not," in Mark's account of the description of hell-fire as given by Jesus (ch. ix. 44, 46, 48), are, strictly speaking, not quite in place.

P. 63 *sq.* ANGELS.—Cornill (*op. cit.*, col. 1682), too, comes to the conclusion that "the conception of angels is, in every respect, genuinely Babylonian." In speaking of "the protecting angels which attend on men" (*cf.*

Ps. xci. 11 *sq.*, Matt. xviii. 10), I had in my mind such passages as that in the well-known Babylonian letter of consolation to the queen-mother from Aplâ (K. 523): "Mother of the king, my lady, be consoled (?)! an angel of grace from Bel and Nebo goes with the king of the lands, my lord"; or that in the writing addressed to Esarhaddon (K. 948): "May the great gods appoint a guardian of health and life at the side of the king, my lord" (similarly 81, 2-4, 75); or, on the other hand, the words of Nabopolassar, the founder of the Chaldæan kingdom: "To the lordship over the land and people Marduk called me. He sent a tutelary deity (Cherub) of grace to go at my side, in everything that I did he made my work to succeed" (see *Mitteilungen der deutschen Orient-Gesellschaft*, No. 10, p. 14 *sq.*).

P. 64. DEVILS.—As distinguished from "the Old Serpent which is the Devil and Satan" (p. 52), in which is preserved the ancient Babylonian conception of Tiâmat, the primæval enemy of the gods, Satan, who appears several times in the later and latest books of the Old Testament, and always as the enemy of man, not of God (see Job, ch. i. *sq.*, 1 Chron. xxi. 1, Zech. iii. 1 *sq.*), owes his origin to the Babylonian belief in demons, which, also, recognised a *ilu limnu* or 'evil god' and a *gallû* or 'devil.'

P. 66. "That such productions of ancient Assyria should thus intrude themselves into our own time," etc. In this connection I should like to draw attention to G. Hellmann's most interesting communication, *Ueber den chaldäischen Ursprung modernen Gewitteraberglaubens* (in the *Meteorologische Zeitschrift*, June 1896, pp. 236–238), where it is shewn that ancient Babylonian weather-lore survives even at the present day in one of the most popular of Swedish chap-books, *Sibyllae Prophetia*, more particularly in a chapter entitled *Tordöns märketecken*—*i.e.*, signs for the weather and fertility throughout the whole year, taken from the thunder in the separate months.

P. 70. 'CANAANITES.'—The term, which was used by me in its usual linguistic sense (see, *e.g.*, Kautzsch, *Hebräische Grammatik*, 27th ed., p. 2), is now replaced in my lecture by 'North Semites,' simply because it has been so frequently misunderstood. A proof that the kings of the first Babylonian dynasty, *Sumu-abi* and his successors, do not belong to that original Semitic stock of Babylonia, Semites mingled with Sumerians, but rather to a later immigrating tribe of Semites, is furnished by the Babylonian scholars themselves, who considered that the names of the two kings *Ḫammurabi* (also *Ammurabi*) and *Ammisadûga* (or *Ammizadûga*) required explanation as being foreign to the language, and rendered the former by *Kimta-rapaštum*, 'widespread family' (*cf.* רְחַבְעָם, Rehoboam), and the latter by *Kimtum-kêttum*, 'upright family' (VR. 44, 21, 22, *a*, *b*). The representation of the ע (in עָם, people, family), by *ḫ* in the name *Ḫammurabi* shows that these Semites, unlike the older stock that had been settled for centuries in Babylonia, still actually pronounced the ע as an ע. Moreover, their pronunciation of *š* as *s* — *Samsu* in *Sa-am-su-ilûna* (*cf.* also *Sumu-abi*) as contrasted with the older Babylonian *Šamšu*—no less than the preformative of the third person of the perfect with *ia* (not *i*)—in the personal names of that time (*Iamlik-ilu*, *Iarbi-ilu*, *Iaḳ-bani-ilu*, etc.)—proves the existence of distinct Semitic tribes, a fact first stated by Hommel and Winckler, which, in spite of Jensen's opposition (*op. cit.*, col. 491), remains irrefutable. Linguistic and historical considerations combine to make it more than probable that these immigrant Semites belonged to the Northern Semites, more precisely to the linguistically so-called "Canaanites" (*i.e.* the Phœnicians, Moabites, Hebrews, etc.), as was first acutely recognised by Hugo Winckler (see his *Geschichte Israels*), who thus makes a particularly important addition to his many valuable services. The *na* of *ilûna* (in *Samsu-ilûna*), which is taken to mean "our God," is not sufficient to prove tribal relationship with Arabia, since, in view of the names *Ammi-zadûga*, *Ammi-ditana*, it is at least equally probable that *ilûna* represents an adjective (note the personal name *I-lu-na* in Meissner's *Beiträge zum altbabyl. Privatrecht*, No. 4; *cf.* אֵלוֹן?). On the other hand, *zadûg*, 'righteous,' may point to a "Canaanite" dialect, both lexically (doubtless = צָדוֹק; for the verbal stem, *cf.* *ṣaduḳ*, 'he is righteous,' in the Amarna tablets), and phonetically (obscuring of *â* to *ô*, *û*; *cf.* *anûki*, 'I,' of the Amarna tablets, etc.); and the same may be said, too, of such contemporary names as *Ia-šú-ub-ilu* (*cf.* Phœn. *Ba-'a-al-ia-šú-bu*, VR, 2, 84). Is Jensen really in a position "to produce an entirely satisfactory explanation from the Babylonian" of such names as *Iašûb-ilu* (col. 491)?

P. 69 *sq.* *Il* אֵל, God.—All Semitic prepositions were originally substantives. As regards the preposition אֶל־, originally *il*, "unto, to, towards," it has not been perceived hitherto that the most probable root-meaning is obviously "turning towards, direction," which has survived in Hebrew, in the phrase, "so and so is לְאֵל יָדְךָ, *i.e.*, at the disposal of thy hand, is in thy power." Here לְאֵל is treated precisely like לִפְנֵי in לְפָנֶיךָ, "at thy disposal" (Gen. xiii. 9), and like the frequently occurring Assyrian *ina pâni*, "at one's disposal." אֶל and פְּנֵי are at times interchanged as synonymous; note the instructive passages, Ps. lxxxiv. 8, on the one hand, and xlii. 3 on the other. The view that אֵל in the above phrase means "power" may be traditional, like a thousand other errors in Hebrew lexicography, but it has never been proved, and for this reason it is not correct to maintain, with König (p. 38), that *ēl* "certainly has some such meaning as power or strength." The only meaning that admits of proof is "turning towards, direction"; by which the concrete meaning, "that towards which a man turns, aim, goal," was at once suggested, *eo ipso* (*cf.* מוֹרָא, fear, and object of fear; חֶמְדָּה, desire, and object of desire, and many others). The Sumerians thought of their gods as dwelling up above in that place to which man turns his eyes, in and above the sky (therefore 𒀭 = "heaven" and "God"), and we ourselves, figuratively, say "heaven" for "God" (*cf.* Dan. iv. 23). A Babylonian psalm, too, calls the Sun-god *digil irṣitim rapaštim*, the "goal of the wide earth," *i.e.*, the goal to which the eyes of all the inhabitants of the earth are turned; and finally the poet in the book of Job (xxxvi. 25), in harmony with a number of other passages from Semitic literature, extols God as the one "on whom hangs everyone's gaze, whom man beholdeth from afar." So, in like manner, the oldest Semites gave to that "God-like" being who was conceived of as dwelling up above in the sky, ruling the heaven and the earth, the name *il*, *ēl*, as that Being to whom their eyes were directed (compare the analogous use of עַל as applied to God and that which appertains to God; Hos. xi. 7).

"The point at which the eye aims," such as the sun or the sky, is, in my opinion, the primary and original meaning of the word, and Oettli (p. 23) is therefore wrong when he supposes that I explain *el* as the "goal for which the human heart yearns," and so "is due to an idea, which is of the nature of a pale philosophical abstraction." Naturally it could not happen otherwise than that the man who sought the deity above with his eyes should also do so with his hands and with his heart at the same time (*cf.* Lament. iii. 41).

Since the meaning "direction, goal" has consequently been proved for *il*, and the use of this word as an appellation of the deity fully accords with Semitic thought, it is inadmissible, therefore, to assume yet another *nomen primitivum—il;* and my statement regarding the divine name *ēl* holds good in every respect. It is quite as useless and illegitimate to find a verb for such a *nom. prim.* as *il* (König, p. 38) as it is to seek a verbal stem for such other primitive biliteral nouns as *jîm*, 'day,' *mŭt*, 'man.' What König (p. 38 *sq.*) adduces besides is not worth refuting. I would note in passing that although I cite Lagarde in my argument for *el* = 'aim,' it is easily perceived that I am quite independent of him—never having read his treatise to the present day; consequently what Jensen, for example, writes (col. 493 *sq.*) against Lagarde's etymology in no way affects my own argument.

But the etymology of the word *il*, *el*, is not the most important feature. The main fact remains that those North Semitic tribes, whom we find settled in North as well as in South Babylonia about 2500 B.C., and whose greatest monarch subsequently was Ḫammurabi (about 2250), thought of and worshipped God as a *single* spiritual Being. (Note that the reference is to that division of the North Semitic tribes who immigrated to Babylonia and later became settled there, not to the Sumero-Semitic Babylonians.)

A number of journals incorrectly attribute to me the view that "even the idea of God among the Jews is to be traced back to Babylonian conceptions of the universe"; and Oettli

(p. 4) wrongly says that according to my view even "the name and worship of Yahwè himself, in conjunction with a more or less clearly developed monotheism, is part of a *Babylonian* inheritance." Similarly, König's question (p. 37): "Does the Old Testament monotheism spring from Babylonia?" with all that is implied in it, rests upon a misapprehension of the words I used in the first edition (p. 46, ll. 11 *sqq.*; p. 47, ll. 12–18), which, I venture to suppose, did not admit of being misunderstood.

Now, as regards those personal names compounded with *il* which are particularly common during the period of the first Babylonian dynasty, it is a fundamental error to maintain with König (pp. 40, 42) that in the case of notorious polytheists the names must be translated and interpreted "*a* God has given," or to ask with Oettli (p. 23): "who can prove that those names are not to be understood from a polytheistic point of view: '*a* God has given,' '*a* God with me'?" Not to mention other reasons, this interpretation is shipwrecked upon such names as *Ilu-amranni* "God, regard me!" *Ilu-tûram* "God, turn again!" and others. Or are we to suppose that such a name as *Bâb-ilu* no longer means "God's gate," but "gate of a God"? No! the age of Ḫammurabi continues to possess those names which are so beautiful and of such importance for the history of religion: *Ilu-ittia* "God with me," *Ilu-amtaḫar* "God I invoke," *Ilu-abi, Ilu-milki* "God is my father, my counsel," *Iarbi-ilu* "great is God," *Iamlik-ilu* "God sits in command," *Ibši-ina-ili* "through God he came into existence," *Avêl-ilu* "servant of God," *Mut(um)-ilu* "man of God" (= Methushael), *Ilûma-le'i* "God is mighty," *Ilûma-abi* "God is my father," *Ilûma-ilu* "God is God," *Šumma-ilu-lâ-ilia* "if God be not my God," etc. Obviously the names are to be judged as a whole. In certain cases (*cf.* also isolated Assyrian names like *Na'id-ilu*), "God" may certainly be regarded simply as an appellative, somewhat after the manner as in the phrase in the Laws of Ḫammurabi, to declare something *maḫar ili* "before God," or in the phrase to swear "by God (*ilu*) and by the king," which appears some hundred times in the contemporary Babylonian contract-tablets (*cf.* 1 Sam. xii. 3, 5, "by Yahwè and by the King"); but viewed as a whole, they make it impossible—it seems to me—for us to think of *ilu* as the "God of the city or of the family" (P. Keil, p. 61), or as the "special tutelary deity" (Zimmern in *KAT*, 3rd ed., second half, p. 354). But it is precisely where "a people who have not been philosophically educated is endeavouring to particularize its terms and concepts and to render them as concretely as possible" (Keil, *op. cit.*, p. 59), that one would necessarily expect to find either the specific name of the deity everywhere intended, or—where the tutelary god of the family or of the newly-born babe is meant—the term "my God" or "his God." An unbiassed and unsophisticated consideration of all these and other names of the time of Ḫammurabi leads one again and again to suppose rather that they took their root in religious ideas which differed from the indigenous polytheistic mode of thought in Babylonia. The character and value of this monotheism cannot be estimated with our present sources of knowledge, but, at the most, they can be inferred from the later development of 'Yahwism.'

P. 70. On p. 46 *sq.* of the first edition I had said, "and since this goal can naturally be only one." On mature reflection these words have been altered into "and since the Divine Essence was viewed by them as a unity."

P. 71. JAHWÈ.—It must be resolutely upheld that, in the two personal names *Ia-a'-ve-ilu* (Bu. 91, 5–9, 314, Rev. 3, see *Cuneiform Texts*, viii. 20), and *Ia-ve-ilu* (Bu. 91, 5–9, 544, l. 4, see *Cuneiform Texts*, viii. 34), the reading *Ia've* is the only possible one in the question. The opposition to my reading—which is incontestable in the present state of our knowledge—has brought to light a lamentable state of ignorance on the part of the critics; and to this also may be ascribed the manifold insinuations in which they have thought they might be allowed to indulge, as, for example, when Prof. Kittel ventures to speak of my reading as "a manœuvre" with a purpose (*als einem tendenziösen "Manöver"*). If only for the sake of checking this exhibition of ignorance, I should like to submit briefly and plainly to my theological critics, and also to one and all of their Assyriological "advisers," the following points. According to my *Assyrische Lesestücken*, 4th ed., p. 27, No. 223, the sign  possesses the following syllabic values: *pi*; *tál*; *tu*; *tam*; in Babylonian, moreover, especially *me/ve*; *mà/và*, *à*; (*vu*); for which it would be better to say *ve*; *và*; *à*; (*vu*). But anyone who has made himself even to a slight extent familiar with the writing of the time of Ḫammurabi, knows (1) that even granted the reading *Ia-'u-mà*, this *mà* can no longer be viewed as the emphatic particle *ma* (so, quite wrongly, König, p. 48 *sq.*, Kittel and others); this is written, without exception, with the usual sign for *ma*, 𒈠. To interpret the names under discussion as "Yes, *Ya'u* is God" is absolutely out of the question. Whoever is disposed to deny this must produce but one example, where the emphatic particle *ma* is written with the sign 𒉿. Moreover, it may be incidentally remarked that the *m* in *Ia-ú-um-ilu* can only be the mimmation, and not the abbreviated *ma*. (2) The reading favoured by C. Bezold: *Ia-'a-bi-ilu* (*ZA* xvi., p. 415 *sq.*) is also impossible, because while in Ḫammurabi's time the sign *bi* 𒁉 also represents the syllable *pi*, conversely, 𒉿 is never used also for *bi*. (3) Further reflection shows, too, that the reading *Ia-(a')-pi-ilu* cannot be considered. The sign 𒉿 is certainly used for *pi* even in Ḫammurabi's time—so several times in the contracts published by Meissner in his *Beiträge zum altbabylonischen Privatrecht* (*e.g. Pi-ir-Ištar*, *Pi-ir-ḫu*, *iḫippi*), and likewise in Ḫammurabi's Law-book (*e.g. upitti*)—but *pi* written 𒁉 is incomparably more frequent, as in the seventy-nine letters of that period published by King, where *pi* is not once rendered by 𒉿, but everywhere by 𒁉. (There is no need here to touch upon the confused remarks by S. Daiches in *ZA* xvi., p. 403 *sq.*) In addition to the above, it is to be added that a "Canaanite" verbal-form *ia'pi*, *ia-pi*, could only be derived from a root הפה or the like, but such a root does not exist. Instead of *Ia(')ve-ilu*, one might even conceivably read *Ia-('a/u-) và/u- ilu*, with radical *v*, but thereby would at once rightly think of recognising in it the god יהוה, the very view which has been rejected. Consequently my reading *Ia-ve-ilu* remains, under the circumstances, the most probable, as also the only one that requires to be taken serious account of.

As regards the *meaning* of the name *Ia(')ve-ilu*, I would express myself with less positiveness than I have done in the case of the *reading*. It is certain that König's proposed interpretation (p. 50 *sq.*): "may God [why not '*a* God'?] protect," from the Arabic *ḥama* "to protect," like Barth's (p. 19) "God grants life" (*Ia-aḫ-ve-ilu*), is in the highest degree improbable. As names of foreign origin they must necessarily have been pronounced *Iaḫve-ilu*, not *Ia've-ilu* or even *Iâve-ilu* (*cf.* *Ra-ḫi-im-ili*), and only at the last extremity could we venture to accept the view that the pronunciation of these foreign personal names had been gradually adapted to Babylonian, and had thereby at once become quite unintelligible. No, if any verbal-form can be supposed to lie in *Ia've*, *Iâve*, it is most reasonable to think of the verb הוה, the older form of היה, presupposed even in Exod. iii. 14, and, with Hommel (p. 11, *cf.* also Zimmern in *Theol. Literaturblatt*, 1902, No. 17, col. 196), to interpret as "God exists." But where in the whole realm of the North Semitic people is there to be found a personal name compounded with הוה, היה (יהי)? There is none! My interpretation "*Ja've* is God" may consequently still be in itself by far the most probable.

But the name of a third man of the same period now comes upon the scene, *Ia-ú-um-ilu* (Bu. 88, 5–12, 329, see *Cuneiform Texts*, iv. 27). In the interests of our science it cannot be too deeply lamented that Hommel (*op. cit.*, p. 11) announces to the world the existence of a Babylonian god "*Iâu* = *Ai*, the moon," a Babylonian or "old Semitic" god, that exists nowhere save in his own imagination. Out of the whole of the Babylonian literature, let Hommel adduce only one single passage where a Babylonian god [il]*Ia* or [il]*Ia-u*, *Ia'u* occurs, and as a name of the moon-god! He cannot do so. *Ia-ú-um-ilu* still remains a name foreign to the language; it belongs to the North Semitic (more precisely, Canaanite) tribes, who have been dealt with above at some length in the notes on pp. 123–129. Among these tribes we find no other god *Ia-ú*, but that same god יָהוּ *Iahû*, whose title is contained in the names *Ia-ú-ḫa-zi* = יְהוֹאָחָז, *Ia-a-ḫu-ú-la-ki-*

im, *Ia-ḫu-ú-na-ta-nu* (in Hilprecht's Murashû & Sons), and others. Now this divine name, *Iahû*, which occurs at the beginning, and especially at the end, of Hebrew personal names, being the shorter form of *Iahve*, *i.e.* "the existing one" (so also Stade, *Lehrbuch der hebräischen Grammatik*, p. 165), presupposes the fuller form. And if even to the Jews of the exilic and post-exilic age the name Yahwè was by no means a *nomen ineffabile*—as the many names of that late period show (*Ia-se-'-ia-a-va* = יְשַׁעְיָהוּ "Isaiah," *Pi-li-ia-a-va* = פְּלָיָה, etc.)—then surely we may even more certainly say that it was not so in that remote age in which the divine name Yahwè was far from possessing that degree of sanctity which it was afterwards to acquire in Israel. The name *Iahum-ilu* accordingly presupposes a fuller name *Ia've-ilu* with the same meaning. And when such a name as *Ia-'-ve-ilu*, *Ia-ve-ilu*, is actually twice attested, should it not be recognized as such—and the more unreservedly since the failure to recognize it by no means gets rid of the existence either of a North Semitic ("Canaanite") divine name Iahû, in every respect identical with Yahwè, or of a name *Iahû-ilu* "Yahu is God," equivalent to the Hebrew יוֹאֵל (Joel), and a thousand years older than the prophet Elijah's watchword on Mount Carmel: "Yahwè is God" (1 Kings xviii. 39)?

That Barth's reading (p. 19), *Ia-ḫu-um-ilu*, which would be an abbreviation of *Ia-aḫ-we-ilu*, is to be rejected *a limine* requires no proof. Even Jensen (*op. cit.*, col. 491 *sq.*) notes that it is "certainly in the highest degree probable that both compounds contain the divine name *Iahveh-Iahu*," and rightly adds: "since then the *Ia'wu* in the name cannot be Assyrian or Babylonian, it is of foreign origin, and consequently the whole name is in all probability 'Canaanite,' and the bearer or bearers of it accordingly 'Canaanite(s).'" He proceeds, however, to say: "But just as one could scarcely conclude from the presence of a Müller or a Schulze in Paris that the Germans were the prevailing people there, so the appearance of a *Ia'wu-il(u)* in Babylonia before 2000 B.C. need not be taken to prove anything beyond the fact that bearers of this name were occasionally able to reach Babylonia." Here I may confidently leave the unprejudiced reader to decide whether the tasty analogy of Müller and Schulze is only remotely justified in view of all such names as *Iarbi-ilu*, *Iamlik-ilu*, etc., mentioned above on p. 70—not to speak of *Ḫammurabi*, *Ammi-zadûga*, etc. Besides, even Jensen himself, as one can see, cannot help leaving the divine name Iahve (Iahvu) attested even before 2000 B.C; *cf.*, too, *Zimmern* (*KAT*, third ed., p. 468 n. 6): "Though a divine name—as is *not unlikely*—may be embodied in *ia-ú-um*, possibly even the name Iahu, Yahwè"—this is sufficient for the present, the acceptance of my reading *Ia-(a'-)ve* and the acknowledgment that my interpretation is correct may follow later.

Accordingly, if the equation *Ia-ú-um* = יָהוּ, יְהוּ, may stand, we are doubly justified in regarding the contemporaneous names *Ilu-idinnam* "God has given," *Šá-ili* "belonging to God," *Ilu-amtaḫar* "God I invoke," *Ilu-tûram* "God, turn again!" etc., as being equivalent, as far as their signification is concerned, to the corresponding Hebrew names אֶלְנָתָן, לָאֵל, שְׁאַלְתִּיאֵל, שׁוּבָאֵל.

TO P. 72. The religion of the immigrant Canaanite tribes quickly gave way before the many-membered Pantheon of the inhabitants of the country, which was of Sumerian origin, and had been established for many centuries.—A similar thing may be observed, almost two thousand years later, in the case of the subjects of the Kingdom of Judah who were transferred to Babylon. It is true that we find often enough in the trade records of Achaemenid times, names of Jewish exiles compounded with *Iâva*—but when the son of one *Malaki-iâva* is called *Nêrgal-Êṭir*, or one *Jašc'-Iâva* (Jesaia) names his daughter *Ṭâbat-(il)-Išḫir*, *i.e.*, "Išḫir (or Ištar) is friendly," it is obvious how great was the influence which the native Babylonian polytheism exerted over all who came within its reach.

P. 75. "Notwithstanding that free and enlightened minds taught openly that Nergal and Nebo, Moon-god and Sun-god, the Thunder-god Ramman, and all other gods were one in Marduk, the god of light."

On these words of mine Jensen (*op. cit.*, col. 493) felt called upon to make the following remarks, which, as might be expected, have been gladly spread abroad by König (p. 43 *sq.*) and others: "This would, of course, be one of the most momentous discoveries that has ever been made in the history of religion, and it is, therefore, extremely regrettable that Delitzsch conceals from us his authority. Nothing of the kind is to be gathered from the texts to which I have had access—that I think I can confidently affirm — and we urgently request him, therefore, as soon as possible, to publish word for word the passage which robs Israel of its greatest glory, in the brilliancy of which it has hitherto shone—that it alone of all nations succeeded in attaining to a pure monotheism." Provided Jensen abides by what he has said, Israel is now indeed robbed of this its greatest glory by the New-Babylonian cuneiform tablet (81, 11—3, 111), which has been made known since its publication in 1895 by Theo. G. Pinches in the *Journal of the Transactions of the Victoria Institute.* Although only fragmentarily preserved, one of the surviving pieces informs us that all, or at any rate the highest, of the deities in the Babylonian Pantheon are designated as one with, and as one in, the god Marduk. I quote here a few lines only :—

ilNin-ib	*Marduk ša alli.*
ilNêrgal	*Marduk ša ḳablu.*
ilZa-má-má	*Marduk ša taḫazi.*
ilBêl	*Marduk ša bêlûtu u mitluktu.*
ilNabû	*Marduk ša nikasi.*
ilSín	*Marduk munammir mûši.*
ilŠamaš	*Marduk ša kênâti.*
ilAddu	*Marduk ša zunnu.*

That is to say (*cf.* the analogous texts II. R. 58, No. 5; II. R. 54, No. 1; III. R. 67, No. 1, etc.), the god Marduk is written and called Ninib, as being Possessor of Power; Nêrgal or Zamama, as being Lord of the Conflict or Battle; Bêl, as being Possessor of Lordship; Nebo, as being Lord of Business (?); Sin, as being Illuminator of the Night; Šamaš, as being Lord of all that is just; and Addu, as being god of Rain. Marduk, accordingly, is Ninib as well as Nergal, Moon-god as well as Sun-god, and so on—the names Ninib and Nergal, Sin and Šamaš are simply different ways of describing the one god Marduk; they are all one, with him and in him. Is not this "Indo-Germanic monotheism, the doctrine of a unity evolving itself out of an original multiplicity"?

Postscript (2nd January 1903).—Jensen's article: *Friedrich Delitzsch und der babylonische Monotheismus*, in the *Christliche Welt*, 1903, No. 1 (1st January), which he himself has just sent me, is wrong from beginning to end. Certainly if the text read *Marduk* [il]*Nin-ib ša alli*—*Marduk* [il]*Nergal ša ḳablu*, etc. But it does not run so! The whole of Jensen's pronouncement seems to me to be a hasty retreat. Let the future decide!

BABEL AND BIBLE

Second Lecture

Delivered before the Members of the Deutsche Orient-Gesellschaft in the presence of the German Emperor

BY

FRIEDRICH DELITZSCH

ORDINARY PROFESSOR OF ORIENTAL PHILOLOGY AND ASSYRIOLOGY IN THE UNIVERSITY OF BERLIN

PREFACE TO LECTURE II

Who is this coming from Edom? in bright-red garments from Boṣra?

Splendid in his raiment, vaunting himself in the fulness of his strength?

"It is I (Yahwè), that speak in righteousness, that am mighty to save!"

Why is there red on thy raiment, and thy garments like his that treadeth the wine-press?

"The wine-press have I trodden alone, and of the peoples there was no man with me,

And I trod them in mine anger and trampled them in my fury,

And their life-stream besprinkled my garments, and all my raiment have I defiled.

For a day of vengeance was in my mind and my year of release had come.

And I looked, because there was no helper, and was stupefied, because there was no supporter.

But mine own arm wrought help for me, and my fury was my support,

And I trod down the peoples in mine anger, and made them drunk with my fury,

And spilled their life-stream on the earth."

Surely, both in diction, style, and spirit a genuine Bedouin battle-song and ode of triumph. No! This passage (Is. lxiii. 1-6), with a hundred others from prophetical literature that are full of unquenchable hatred directed against surrounding peoples—against Edom and Moab, Assyria and Babylon, Tyre and Egypt—that for the most part, too, are masterpieces of Hebrew rhetoric, must represent the ethical prophets and prophecy of Israel, even at their most advanced stage! The outcome of certain definite events, these outbursts of political jealousy and of a passionate hatred, which, judged from the human standpoint, may, perhaps, be quite natural and comprehensible enough — such outbursts on the part of generations long since passed away must still do duty for us children of the twentieth century after Christ, for the Christian peoples of the West, as a Book of Religion, for morality, and for edification! Instead of immersing ourselves in "thankful wonder" at the providential guidance shewn by God in the case of our own people, from the earliest times of primitive Germany until to-day, we persist — either from ignorance, indifference, or infatuation — in ascribing to those old-Israelitish oracles a 'revealed' character which cannot be maintained, either in the light of science, or in that of religion or ethics. The more deeply I immerse myself in the spirit of the prophetic literature of the Old Testament, the greater becomes my mistrust of Yahwè, who butchers the peoples with the sword of his insatiable anger; who has but one favourite child, while he consigns all other nations to darkness, shame, and ruin; who uttered those words to Abraham (Gen. xii. 3):

"I will bless those who bless thee, and those who curse thee will I curse"—I take refuge in Him who, in life and death, taught: "Bless those who curse you"; and, full of confidence and joy, and of earnest striving after moral perfection, put my trust in the God to Whom Jesus has taught us to pray—the God Who is a loving and righteous Father over all men on earth.

FRIEDRICH DELITZSCH.

CHARLOTTENBURG,
1st March 1903.

LECTURE II

WHAT good purpose is served by the onslaught directed against the choice of "Babel and Bible" as a title, since logic, at any rate, imperatively demands such a sequence of terms? And how can anyone imagine it possible to ban discussion of these grave and—so far as the Bible is concerned—all-embracing questions with the shibboleth of 'original revelation,' discredited as the latter term already is by a forgotten verse[1] of the Old Testament? Moreover, does "the ethical monotheism of Israel" in its essential character as "a real revelation of the living God" really form, after all, such an unassailable, such a triumphant bulwark, in the intellectual conflict which Babylon has kindled in our days? It is certainly a pity that so many people should

[1] See p. 207.

allow the joy naturally felt over the rich harvest that Babylon is continually offering for the 'elucidation and illustration' of the Bible, to be turned into gall and bitterness by a prejudiced regard for dogmatic considerations—to the extent, indeed, of ignoring its value and utility altogether. And yet what a debt of gratitude has been laid upon all readers and interpreters of the Bible for the new knowledge already

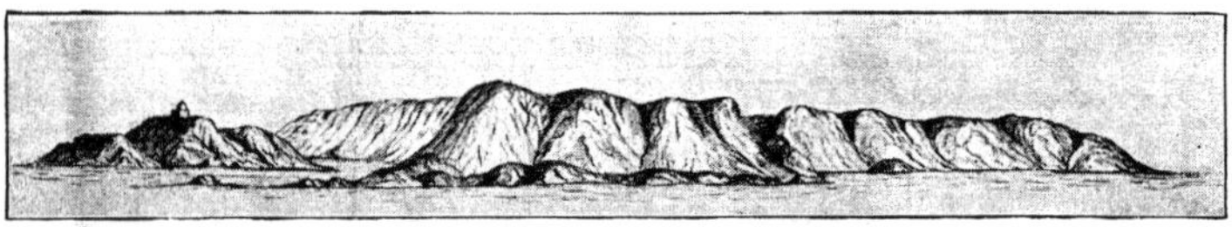

Fig. 52.—Ruin-mounds of Cuthah.

made—and continually being made—available for us by the laborious excavations on the sites of Babylonian and Assyrian ruins!

For my own part, I avoid, on principle, ever speaking of 'corroborations' of the Bible. For in truth the Old Testament would be badly served as a source of ancient history if it first needed corroboration at every turn by the cuneiform monuments. When, however, the Biblical book of Kings informs us (2 Kings xvii. 30) that the inhabitants of a certain town Cuthah, who had been settled in Samaria, worshipped the god Nergal—and when we now not only know

Fig. 53.—Assyrian letter from Chalach.

that this Babylonian town of Cuthah lies buried beneath the rubbish-mound of Tell Ibrahim (fig. 52), seven hours' journey north-west of Babylon, but also that a cuneiform text expressly declares that the local deity of Cuthah was called Nergal, it is something to be grateful for: and though there seemed small likelihood that the city and district of Chalach, to which a portion of the Israelites taken captive by Sargon were transplanted

Fig. 54.—The Black Obelisk of Salmanassar II. (860–825 B.C.).

(2 Kings xvii. 6, xviii. 11), would ever be discovered, yet it is worth noting that we now possess out of Ashur-bani-pal's library at Nineveh a letter from Chalach (fig. 53), in

which a certain Marduk-nadin-acḫi, emphasizing his proved unbroken loyalty, prays the king to procure the restoration to him of

Figs. 55 and 56.—Israelites of the time of Jehu (840 B.C.).

his estate, which the king's father had presented to him, and which had afforded him the means of livelihood during fourteen years, until he had been deprived of it lately by the governor of the land Mašḫalzi. With respect to the inhabitants of the northern Israelitish kingdom, whom the famous Black Obelisk of

Figs. 57 and 58.—Israelites of the time of Jehu (840 B.C.).

Shalmaneser II. (fig. 54) brings so vividly before our eyes in its second tier of bas-reliefs (figs. 55–58)—they are the ambassadors of King

Jehu (840 B.C.) with various sorts of presents. We now know all three districts where the Ten Tribes found their grave: Chalach somewhat east of the mountainous region, named Arrapachitis, where the sources of the upper Zab take their rise; the district of Gozan on the bank of the Chabor, in the neighbourhood of Nisibis; and the towns of Media. Until quite recently the capture and sack of the Egyptian Thebes mentioned by the prophet Nahum (ch. iii. 8 *sqq.*) remained a riddle, in so far that no one was able to say to what event the prophet's words had reference: "Art thou (Nineveh) better than No-Amon (*i.e.* Thebes), that lies among the Nile-streams, (that has) the water round about her . . .? She also had to go into captivity, her children also were dashed to pieces at the corners of all streets, and over her honourable men they cast the lot, and all her magnates were bound with chains." Then came the discovery at Nineveh of the magnificent decagonal clay prism of Ashur-bani-pal (fig. 59), which in its second column narrates that it was Ashur-bani-pal who, while on the way from Memphis in hot pursuit of the Egyptian King Urdamanê, reached Thebes, sacked it, and carried away from Thebes to Nineveh, the city of his sovereignty, silver, gold, precious stones, the whole of the palace-treasures, the inhabi-

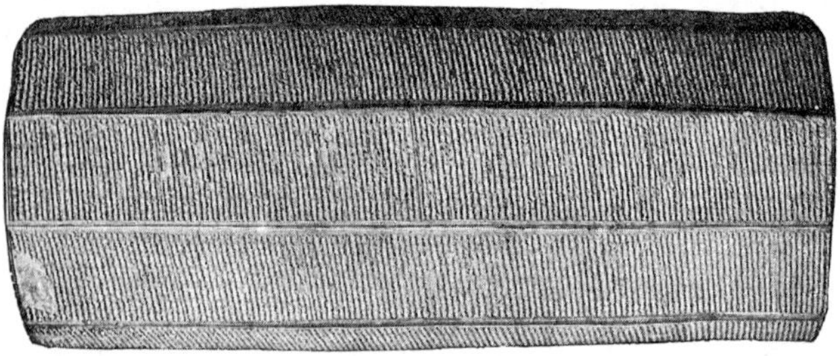

Fig. 59.—Decagonal clay prism of Ashur-bani-pal.

tants, men and women—a vast, immeasurable booty.

Then, again, how great a service has been rendered by the cuneiform literature for the elucidation of the language of the Old Testament! The Old Testament repeatedly mentions an animal called *re'ēm*, a wild untamable creature, equipped with terrible horns (Ps. xxii. 22), nearly related to the bull (Deut. xxxiii. 17; Ps. xxix. 6; *cf.* Isaiah xxxiv. 7), the idea of employing which like a tame ox for the work of the fields is to the author of the Book of Job (xxxix. 9 *sqq.*) something altogether terrible and inconceivable: "Will the *re'ēm* be content to serve thee, or will he lodge in thy crib? Canst thou bind the *re'ēm* with the guiding-rope in thy furrow, or will he harrow the valleys after thee?" Though the buffalo roams in herds about the woods on the farther side of the Jordan at the present day, it was not until shortly before the commencement of our era that the species migrated from Arachosia to hither Asia; it has therefore been customary, on the strength of a comparison with the Arabic *usus loquendi*, which designates the antelope 'wild ox,' and bestows on the antelope leukoryx the name of *ri'm*, to understand by the Hebrew *re'ēm* this particular kind of antelope. How it could have occurred to a poet, however, to imagine this creature (fig. 60)—which, in spite of its long, pointed horns, is still only a delicately formed, tender-eyed antelope—as yoked to a plough, and then to shudder at the very thought of such a thing, was not explained. The cuneiform inscriptions have taught us

Fig. 60.—Antelope leukoryx.

what the *rêmu* really was: it was a powerful, fierce-looking wild ox, equipped with strong curved horns, an animal of the forest and the mountain, accustomed to scale the peaks of the highest hills, a creature endowed with immense bodily strength, to hunt which, as in the case of the lion, was by reason of its dangerous character a favourite pastime of the Assyrian monarchs. The existence of this animal, which is nearly related to the *bos urus* of Cæsar (*Bell. Gall.*, vi. 28), as well as to the bison, is, so far as the district of the Lebanon is concerned, made certain by natural history;

Fig 61.—Assyrian representation of the wild ox (Re'ēm).

the cuneiform inscriptions make mention of the *re'ēm* times without number, and the alabaster reliefs of the Assyrian royal palaces (fig. 61) set it before our eyes in palpable shape. In the matter of the *re'ēm* the German Oriental Society has earned special distinction. For King Nebuchadnezzar relates that he adorned the city-gate of Babylon, which was dedicated to the goddess Ishtar, with bricks, on which *rêmu* and immense serpents, standing erect, were depicted: and the recovery of this Ishtar-Gate, together with the work of laying it bare to a depth of fourteen metres, where the water-level begins, constitutes one of the

Fig. 62.—Bâbil, the northernmost ruin-mound of Babylon.

most important achievements of recent years in our excavations on the site of Babylon.

Hail to thee, O mound of Bâbil (fig. 62), to thee and thy companions on the palm-girt banks of Euphrates! How the pulses quicken when, after long weary weeks of work with pick and spade, under the scorching rays of an

Eastern sun, the long-sought building is disclosed—when, inscribed on an immense slab of stone, the name 'Ishtar-Gate' is read, and, piece by piece, the great double-gate of Babylon, flanked northward by three mighty towers, emerges from the bowels of the earth in splendid preservation. Whichever way we look, on the wall-surfaces of the towers as well as of the Gateway-passages, every part swarms with reliefs, *rêmu* coloured on their surface with enamels standing out against the background of deep blue (fig. 63). "Mightily the wild ox strides with long step, and neck proudly raised, with horns bent threateningly forward, ears turned back, nostrils dilated; the muscles tense and swollen, the tail lifted and falling away in a vigorous curve—all as nature dictates, yet enhanced by an air of nobility." If the smooth skin is white, the horns and hoofs are of a brilliant golden hue; if the skin is yellow, then both are of malachite-green, while the mane in each case is painted a deep blue. Of truly noble appearance, however, is a white bull in relief, of which not merely the horns and hoofs, but the mane as well, are painted sap-green.

Such is the *re'ēm* of the Gate of Ishtar, through which the Procession-Street of Marduk led, a worthy companion to the well-known

Fig. 63.—The wild ox (Re'ēm), relief in enamelled bricks from Babylon.

"lion of Babylon" (fig. 64), which adorned that famous street.

And besides this, the German Oriental Society has also presented Biblical Science with another animal of the rarest kind, with a fabulous beast which our religious training has made us well acquainted with, and which must make a fascinating impression on all who approach the Palace of Nebuchadnezzar through the Ishtar-Gate—I mean the *Dragon of Babel* (fig. 65).

"With neck extended far forward, and

Fig. 64.—The "lion of Babylon."

poison-threatening glance, the monster strides along"—it is a serpent, as the long double-tongued head, the long scaly body, and the serpentine tail clearly shew; but it also, at the same time, possesses the fore-legs of the panther, while its hind legs are armed with immense talons; and in addition it carries long straight horns on the head, and a scorpion-sting at the end of the tail.[1] All, all be thanked, who faithfully and truly co-operate for the acquisition of such choice, and archæologically all-important, discoveries!

Fig. 65.—The dragon of Babel.

But quite apart from many such explanatory and illustrative details, Assyriology has re-established the credit of *The Tradition of the Old Testament Text*, which has so long and so fiercely been assailed. For while

[1] See Note, p. 221.

Assyriology is itself ever being confronted by newly-discovered texts of growing difficulty, full of rare words and modes of speech, it can understand that within the Old Testament Scriptures also there are plenty of words and expressions that occur but once or rarely; it rejoices in the fact, and makes it its business to attempt to explain such from the context, and, in not a few cases, reaps the reward of its labour by discovering the occurrence of the self-same words and phrases in Assyrian. It perceives in this way how fatal a mistake it has been for modern exegesis to quibble about such rare words and difficult passages, to 'emend' them, and only too often to substitute platitudes. In truth, every friend of the Old Testament Scriptures should strenuously co-operate in contributing to help unearth the thousands of clay-tablets and all the other sorts of literary monuments which lie buried in Babylon, and which our Expedition will set to work to excavate, as soon as the initial tasks that have been imposed upon it have been successfully discharged. By so doing, he will help to promote a more notable and rapid advance in the linguistic elucidation of the Old Testament than has been possible for two thousand years.

Even whole narratives of the Old Testament receive their elucidation from Babylon. From youth we have been burdened by tradition with the false notion of a brutalized Nebuchadnezzar, because the Book of Daniel narrates (ch. iv. 29–37) how the King of Babel wandered about on the roof of his palace, and, after glorying again in the majesty of the city he had built, was the recipient of a prophecy from Heaven to the effect that he should be driven out from human society, and should live with and after the manner of the beasts of the field. Thereupon, we are told, King Nebuchadnezzar did eat grass in the wilderness like the oxen, wet with the dew of heaven, while his hair grew like eagles' feathers, and his nails like birds' claws. Yet no instructor of youth, at least since the appearance of Eberhard Schrader's essay, "Concerning the Madness of Nebuchadnezzar,"[1] ought ever to have taught this story without pointing out that the purer and more original form of it has long been known to us in a Chaldæan legend preserved in Abydenus. This story narrates that Nebuchadnezzar, having attained the summit of his power, ascended the roof of the royal castle, and, inspired by a god, cried out and said: "I, Nebuchadnezzar (Nabukodrosor), announce to you the coming of a calamity which neither Bel nor queen Beltis can persuade the Fates to avert. There shall come a Persian (*i.e.* Cyrus) . . . . and bring you into slavery. Would that, before the citizens perish, he might be hunted through the desert where neither city nor track of man could be found, but where rather wild beasts seek their food, and birds fly; would that among mountain clefts and gorges he might wander alone. But as for me . . . . may I encounter a happier end." Who could fail to observe here

[1] See Note, p. 221.

that the Hebrew writer has freely altered the Babylonian legend, especially since in verse 19 he lets it clearly be seen that he was quite well acquainted with its original wording! What Nebuchadnezzar desires for the enemy of the Chaldæans, the author of the collection of pamphlets (which abound in mistakes and omissions) embodied in the Book of Daniel attributes to the experience of Nebuchadnezzar himself, in order to bring home by concrete example, and in the strongest possible manner, to his countrymen, persecuted by Antiochus Epiphanes, the truth that the Lord God can utterly abase even the most powerful king who resists Yahwè.

When shall we at last learn to distinguish, within the Old Testament, form from substance? There are two profound lessons that the author of the Book of Jonah preaches to us—viz., that no one can escape God, and that no mortal may dare attempt to regulate or even set a limit to God's compassion or long-suffering; but the form in which these truths are clothed is human, altogether and fantastically Oriental; and if we at this time of day were willing to believe that Jonah in the fish's belly uttered a prayer made up of a mosaic of Psalm-passages which were composed in part some centuries after the fall of Nineveh, or that the King of Nineveh's repentance was so profound that he commanded even the oxen and sheep to clothe themselves with sackcloth, we should ourselves be sinning against the intelligence that God has bestowed upon us. But all such features are mere details that fade into the background before the far intenser light.

It was a remarkably happy idea which was conceived by the representatives of the governing bodies of the German churches, who went out to Jerusalem as the Kaiser's guests to be present at the dedication of the Church of the Redeemer—the idea of founding a "German Evangelical Institute of Archæology for the Holy Land."

Oh, may our young theologians there learn

to acquaint themselves thoroughly—and that not merely in the towns, but, best of all, in the desert—with the manners and customs of the Bedouin, who are still the self-same people that they were in the time of old Israel; and may they there deeply immerse themselves in the points of view and modes of presentment characteristic of the Orient: may they listen, in the tents of the desert, to story-tellers, or hear the descriptions and narrations of the sons of the desert themselves, full of vivid and unrestrained, spontaneous fancy, which all too often unwittingly transgresses the limits of fact! There will then be disclosed to them that world from which alone Oriental works like the Old and (to some extent also) the New Testament can be explained—there will fall as it were scales from their eyes, and the "Midnight Sun"[1] will be transformed into morning light!

If even the Orient of to-day—wherever we go and stay, listen and look—offers such an

[1] See Note, p. 222.

abundance of elucidatory material for the Bible, how much more must this be true of the study of the ancient literature of the Babylonians and Assyrians, which indeed is to some extent contemporary with the Old Testament! Everywhere we meet with more or less significant agreements on the part of the two literatures, which are closely related in respect of language and style, thought and modes of presentment. I call to mind the sacred character of the numbers seven and three, to which both testify. "O Land, Land, Land, hear the word of Yahwè," cries Jeremiah (ch. xxii. 29); "Hail, hail, hail to the King, my Lord" is the formula with which more than one Assyrian scribe begins his letter. And just as the Seraphim before God's Throne cry, one to the other: "Holy, holy, holy is Yahwè Sabaoth" (Is. vi. 3), so we read at the beginning of the Assyrian Temple-liturgies a thrice-repeated *ašur*, *i.e.*, 'Salvation-bringing' or 'holy.' According to Babylonian ideas magic power belongs in a special degree to human spittle. Spittle and magic form closely connected ideas, and in fact spittle was regarded as possessing death-bringing as well as life-bestowing force. "O Marduk!"—runs a petition in a prayer to the city-deity of Babel —"O Marduk! To thee belongs the spittle of life!" Who can fail in such a connection to recall New Testament accounts such as that which narrates that Jesus took the deaf and dumb man aside, put his fingers into his ears, spat, and with the spittle touched his tongue, and said: "*Ephphatha*," "Be thou opened!" (Mark vii. 33 *sqq.*; *cf.* viii. 23; John ix. 6 *sqq.*) With a pillar of smoke by day, and a pillar of fire by night, Yahwè accompanied his people on the journey through the desert; but to Esarhaddon also, the King of Assyria, there is given, before his departure for the war, the prophetic assurance: "I, Ishtar of Arbela, will make to ascend on thy right hand smoke, and on thy left hand fire." "Set thy house in order"—says the prophet Isaiah to King

Hezekiah, who is sick unto death—"because thou art dead, and shalt not live" (Is. xxxviii. 1); and the Assyrian general Kudurru, to whom the King despatches His Majesty's physician-in-ordinary, thanks his King with the words: "I was dead, but the King, my Lord, has made me live" (K. 81, 12). The soul of one who is sick unto death dwells already in the under-world, has journeyed already down to the grave (Ps. xxx. 3). Therefore the goddess Gula, the patroness of physicians, bears the title of "Awakener of the Dead"; an Oriental physician, who did not awaken the dead, would be regarded as no physician. How utterly alike everything is in Babylon and Bible! Here as there we are struck by the fondness shewn for illustrating speech and thought by symbolic action (I call to mind the scapegoat which was driven into the wilderness): here as there we meet with the same world of perpetual wonders and signs; of continuous revelation, principally in dreams; the same naïve representations of the godhead;—just as in Babylon the gods eat and drink, and even betake themselves to rest, so Yahwè goes forth in the cool of the evening to walk in Paradise, and takes pleasure in the sweet scent of Noah's sacrifice; and just as in the Old Testament Yahwè speaks to Moses and Aaron, and to all the prophets, so the gods in Babylon spoke to men, either directly or through the mouth of their priests and inspired prophets and prophetesses.

Revelation indeed! A greater mistake on the part of the human mind can hardly be conceived than this, that for long centuries the priceless remains of the old Hebrew literature collected in the Old Testament were regarded collectively as a religious canon, a revealed book of religion, in spite of the fact that it includes such literature as the Book of Job, which, with words that in places border on blasphemy, casts doubts on the very existence of a just God, together with absolutely secular productions, such as wedding songs (the so-called Song of Solomon). In the charming love-song, Ps. xlv., we read, vv. 11 *sqq.*: "Hearken, O daughter, and attend, and incline thine ear, and forget thine own people and thy father's house; and should the king long for thy beauty, for he is thy lord, then prostrate thyself before him."

The thought may suggest itself, what must have been the result when books and passages like these were interpreted theologically, and even messianically (*cf.* Ep. to Hebrews i. 8 *sq.*)? It can hardly have been otherwise than with the mediæval Catholic monk, who, if he met with the Latin word *maria*, 'seas,' while reading in the Psalter, crossed himself in honour of the Virgin Mary. But even for the remaining portions of the Old Testament literature, all scientifically trained theologians, Evangelical as well as Catholic, have abandoned the doctrine of verbal inspiration: the Old Testament is itself responsible for this, with its numberless contradictory double narratives, and with the absolutely inextricable confusion that has arisen in the five books of Moses, through constant revision and interchange.

To be quite frank, beyond the revelation of God that we, each one of us, carry in our own conscience, we have certainly not deserved a further personal Divine revelation. For up to this day mankind has absolutely trifled with the original and most special revelation of the holy God, the ten words written on the Tables of the Law from Sinai. "The Word ye shall let stand"; in spite of this, in Dr Martin Luther's Small Catechism, according to which our children are instructed, the whole of the second commandment: "Thou shalt not make to thyself any image or likeness," has been suppressed, and in place of it the last commandment, or rather negative command, concerning the so-called evil desire has been severed into two parts, a division which could easily be seen to be inadmissible from a comparison of Exodus xx. 17 and Deut. v. 18. Thus the commandment to honour father and mother is made to be not the fourth, but the fifth, and so on.

And in the Roman Catholic catechism, which has exactly the same numeration of the Ten Commandments, the first commandment appears in an expanded form, and runs thus: "Thou shalt have no strange gods beside me; thou shalt not make to thyself any graven image to worship it"; but immediately after this it is added: *Images of Christ, of the Mother of God, and of all Saints we nevertheless make, because we do not worship, but only honour them*—in which connection it has been overlooked that the Lord God says expressly: *Thou shalt not make to thyself any graven image to worship and to honour it.* (See also Deut. iv. 16.)

But the case is even worse if, for the time being, we assume the standpoint of the strict letter of the law; for then Moses himself will have to bear the terrible reproach—a reproach ascending in one unanimous shriek from all peoples of the earth, who ask and seek after God. Let it be remembered, it is Almighty God, "the All-embracing, All-sustaining," the

Invisible, the Unapproachable One, who, amid thunder and lightning, from the midst of cloud and fire, announces His most holy will; Yahwè, "the Rock whose deeds are perfect" (Deut. xxxii. 4), it is who chisels with His own hands two tables of stone and engraves on them with His own fingers, which hold the world in equilibrium, the Ten Commandments—then Moses in a fit of anger hurls the eternal tables of the eternal God from him, and shivers them into a thousand fragments. Further, this God writes a second time other tables which set forth His first and last autograph revelation to mankind, God's unique palpable revelation, and Moses does not think it worth while to impart to his people, and thereby to mankind, a literal and exact account of what God engraved on those tables.

We scholars would count it a grave reproach to any one of ourselves to render falsely or inaccurately, even in a single letter, the inscription of any one, even a herdsman, who had perpetuated his name on a stone of the

Sinaitic peninsula; but Moses, when he once more, before the crossing of the Jordan, inculcates the Ten Commandments to his people, not only changes individual words, transposes words and clauses and more of the like, but even replaces one long passage by another, although he emphatically and expressly asserts that this also corresponds to the very letter of God's words. And so to this day we know not whether God commanded the Sabbath Day to be hallowed in remembrance of His own rest after the six days' work of creation (Ex. xx. 11; *cf.* xxxi. 17), or as a memorial of the unending compulsory labour of the people during their sojourn in Egypt (Deut. v. 14 *sq.*). And the same remissness in regard to God's most holy testament to men is also to be deplored in other respects. We are still seeking for the mountain in the Sinai range which corresponds in all respects with what the account tells us; and while we are most fully informed about numberless trifling details, such as, for example, the rings and rods of the chest which served to protect the two tables,—with regard to their external appearance and character, apart from the fact that they had writing on both sides, we learn nothing whatever.

When the Philistines capture the Ark of the Covenant and bring it into the temple of Dagon at Ashdod, on the very next morning the image of the god Dagon lies shattered before the Ark of Yahwè (1 Sam. v. *sqq.*). When after this it is brought to the little Jewish frontier hamlet of Beth-Shemesh, and the inhabitants peep at it, seventy—according to another account 50,000 (!)—men pay the penalty with death (1 Sam. vi. 19). Even one who touches the Ark by mistake is slain by Yahwè's wrath (2 Sam. vi. 7 *sq.*). As soon, however, as we set foot on the firm ground of historical times, history is silent. We are informed in minute detail that the Chaldæans carried off the Temple treasures of Jerusalem, and the gold, silver, and copper vessels of the Temple, the basins and bowls and shovels (2 Kings xxiv. 13, xxv. 13 *sqq.*), but for the

Ark, with the two divine Tables, nobody inquires ; the Temple perishes in flames, but to the fate of the two wonder-working Tables of Almighty God—of this greatest of the sacred possessions of the Old Covenant—there is devoted not a single word.

We will not stop to investigate the cause of all this, but will only point out that Moses is acquitted by Pentateuchal criticism of the reproach which, according to the strict letter of the law, lies upon him. For, as, in company with many other scholars, Dillmann (*Kommentar zu den Büchern Exodus und Leviticus*, p. 201)—who is esteemed as an authority even on the Catholic side—clearly establishes, the Ten Commandments lie before us in two different Recensions, which do not go back immediately to the tables but to other and distinct categories. And in the same way also all the other so-called Mosaic laws have been handed down to us in two relatively late Recensions, which for centuries existed independently in distinct forms ; and by this means all differences receive their explanation easily enough. Moreover, we also know this, that the so-called Mosaic laws, institutions, and customs exhibit those elements which partly from a long antiquity possessed validity among the Children of Israel, but partly also only secured valid recognition after the settlement of the people in Canaan, and were then referred back *en bloc* to Moses, and, with a view to enhancing their sacred character and inviolability, to Yahwè himself, as the supreme Lawgiver. We observe exactly the same process at work in the laws of other old peoples—I recall, at the moment, the law-book of Manu—and the case is exactly the same with the giving of the law among the Babylonians.

When, last year, I had the honour of speaking in this place, I pointed out that we find a highly-developed organization of law already in existence in Babylonia about 2250 B.C.,[1] and I spoke of a great collection of laws of Ḫammurabi, which determines the civil law in all

[1] See p. 35.

its departments. What could then only be inferred from scattered though unmistakable details—viz., the existence of such a code—has now been demonstrated by the discovery of Ḫammurabi's great Law-Book in the original; and by this great find science, and particularly the history of culture, and comparative jurisprudence, have been enriched with a treasure of the utmost value. It was among the ruins of the Acropolis of Susa that at the end of the year 1901 and the beginning of 1902 the French archæologist de Morgan and the Dominican monk Scheil had the good fortune to find a diorite block of King Ḫammurabi, 2½ metres high, which had obviously been carried off with other war-booty from Babylon by the Elamites; and on it were found engraved, in the most careful manner, 282 paragraphs of laws (fig. 66). They consist, as the King himself says, of "Laws of righteousness, which Ḫammurabi, the mighty and just King, has established for the advantage and benefit of the weak and oppressed, the widows

Fig. 66.—A small portion of the inscription of the Laws of Ḫammurabi.

and orphans." "Let the wronged," we read, "who has a lawsuit, read this my written monument, and examine my precious words; let my written monument explain to him the position of the law, and let him see the decision of it! With heart breathing freely again, let him then exclaim: 'Ḫammurabi is a Lord who is like a just father to his people.'"

But though the King says that he, the Sun of Babylon, the Light streaming over south and north of his land, has written down these laws, yet he, on his part, has received them from the supreme Judge of Heaven and Earth, the Possessor of everything that is just and right, the Sun-god; and therefore the mighty Law-Stone bears on its summit the beautiful bas-relief (fig. 67) showing Ḫammurabi as he receives the revelation of the laws from Shamash, the supreme Law-giver.

With the giving of the Law from Sinai, the conclusion of a so-called covenant by Yahwè with Israel, it is in no respect different. In spite of this sacrosanct bond the purely human origin and character of the Israelitish Law is sufficiently obvious! Or, would any one have the temerity to assert that the thrice-holy God, who with his own fingers engraved on the table of stone the words *lô tiḳtōl,*

Fig. 67.—Ḫammurabi receiving the Laws from the Sun-god.

"Thou shalt not kill," could in the very same breath have sanctioned Blood-Revenge, which to this day lies like a curse on the peoples of the East, especially as Ḫammurabi had already "almost wholly eradicated all traces of it"? Or, would any one be found ready to cling to the notion that circumcision, which has been customary from ancient times among the Egyptians and Arabian Bedouin, is the sign of a special covenant of God with Israel? In accordance with Oriental modes of thought and speech, we can very well understand the fact that the numerous prescriptions for all possible—even the minutest—events of daily life (as, for instance, in the case when a vicious ox gores a human being, or another ox, to death: Exodus xxi. 28 *sq.*, 35 *sq.*), the dietary laws, the minute medical regulations governing diseases of the skin, the directions respecting the priestly wardrobe, were represented as proceeding from Yahwè himself; but all this is purely external setting—the God to whom the most acceptable sacrifices are "a broken spirit, a broken and contrite heart" (Ps. li. 17), and who took no delight in a sacrificial worship after the manner of the 'heathen' peoples (Ps. xl. 6), is certainly not to be credited with having devised recipes for anointing-oil and frankincense, "after the art of the perfumer," as the expression runs (Exod. xxx. 25, 35). It will be a matter for future investigation to determine how far the Israelitish laws—civil as well as priestly—are specifically Israelitish or are common to Semitic races generally, or whether they have been influenced by the far older Babylonian legislation, which certainly had spread beyond the boundaries of Babylonia itself. I call to mind, for example, the *lex talionis*—eye for eye, tooth for tooth—the festivals of the new moon, the 'shew-bread,' so-called, the High Priest's breast-plate, and many other features.

Meanwhile we should be thankful that it has been recognised that the institution of the Sabbath Day, the origin of which was obscure even to the Hebrews, has its roots in the Babylonian *šabattu*, the 'Day' *par excellence.* On the other hand, nobody asserts that the Ten Commandments were borrowed, even partially, from Babylonia; stress rather is laid on pointing out that such Commandments as the fifth, sixth, and seventh owe their origin to an instinct of self-preservation common to the human race. As a matter of fact, the majority of the Ten Commandments were as sacred to the Babylonians as to the Hebrews: disrespect shewn towards parents, false witness, any and every attempt to secure other people's property, were, according to Babylonian custom, sternly punished, for the most part with death. So, for example, we read as third paragraph of Ḫammurabi's Law-Book: "If any one in a law-suit makes lying depositions, and cannot prove his assertions, he shall, if thereby the life of another is endangered, be punished with death." Quite specifically Israelitish is the second Commandment, the prohibition of every form of image-worship whatever, which seems to have a directly anti-Babylonian point. In coming to the consideration of the first Commandment — so thoroughly Israelitish in character:—"I am Yahwè, thy God, thou shalt have none other Gods beside me," I may be permitted to approach more closely a point about which all who interest themselves in the problems of Babel and Bible manifest a persistent and profound concern—I mean the question of Old Testament Monotheism. It is, after all, quite comprehensible, from the standpoint of Old Testament Theology, that after having unanimously abandoned—and rightly so—the doctrine of the verbal inspiration of the Old Hebrew Writings, and after acknowledging (albeit unwillingly, yet quite consistently) the absolutely non-binding character of the Old Testament Scriptures as such upon our faith, knowledge, and recognition, it should now claim that their pervading spirit is divine, and, with so much the greater insistence, should emphasize the ethical monotheism of Israel, the "spirit of the prophets," as being "a real revelation of the living God."

The effect of the proper names, enumerated in my last year's lecture,[1] which we find to have been current in immensely large numbers

[1] See p. 70.

among the North Semitic Nomads, who, about 2500 B.C., had wandered into Babylonia, has proved quite startling—names such as "El, *i.e.* God, has given," "God sits enthroned in power," "If God be not my God," "God! behold me!" "God is God," "Jahu (*i.e.* Jahve) is God." The uneasiness produced by this catalogue is really not quite comprehensible. Since the Old Testament itself already allows Abraham to preach in Jahve's name (Gen. xii. 8), and Jahve is already the God of Abraham, Isaac, and Jacob, such old names as *Jahu-ilu*, *i.e.* Joel, should really be hailed with joy. And more particularly in the case of those theologians who claim to be positive, who allow that "all divine revelation develops, stage by stage, historically"—thereby, as it seems to me, entirely contradicting the Church's idea of revelation—should the advent of these names be opportune. Meanwhile the great majority of theologians have an uneasy feeling, and with reason, that these names, which are something like a thousand years or more older than the corresponding Old Testament names, and which testify to the worship of only one God (whether tribal god or otherwise is a matter of opinion) named Jahu, "the Abiding One," may involve the transference of the starting-point for the historical development of Jahve-religion to very much wider circles than those having a special place within the ranks of Abram's descendants, thereby, however, gravely endangering its character as a revelation. And therefore no efforts, no pains are spared to explain these names away, no means being rejected for this end—but even though the waves sputter and foam, the names of the descendants of the North Semitic Bedouin, dating from *circa* 2300 B.C., remain, like a lighthouse in a dark night, firm and immovable: "God is God," "Jahu is God."

It seems to me that, both on the one side and the other, people need to be on their guard against exaggeration. For my own part, I have never failed to emphasize the 'coarseness' of the polytheism of the Babylonians, and I do not feel myself constrained in the least to palliate it. Only, I regard the Sumerian-Babylonian Pantheon and its representation in poetry (especially in popular poetry) as quite as little suited to be the butt of shallow criticisms and mocking exaggerations as the Homeric gods, similar ridicule of whom would be properly condemned. Nor should the worship of the deities under forms of stone and wood be in any way extenuated. Only, it should never be forgotten that even according to the biblical account of creation, man is created in the very image of God ; and this feature, as has rightly been emphasized already from the theological side, directly contradicts the other aspect of God which is repeatedly laid stress upon—His immateriality.

So it is, after all, not altogether incomprehensible if the Babylonians, reversing the process, set forth and represented their gods in human likeness. The Old Testament prophets do exactly the same thing, at least in the spirit. In complete agreement with Babylonian and Assyrian representations, the prophet Habakkuk (ch. iii.) sees Yahwè approach with horses and chariots, bow and arrows, and lance, and even (ver. 4) "horns at His side"—yes, with horns, the symbol of supremacy,

Fig. 68.—Assyrian god with "horns at its side."

strength, and victory (Amos vi. 13; *cf.* Numb. xxiii. 22), the usual decoration of the head-covering (fig. 68) of the Babylonian-Assyrian gods, both high and low. The representations of God the Father in Christian Art; in the case of Michael Angelo, Raphael, in all our picture Bibles—the accompanying representation (fig. 69) of the fourth day of creation is taken from that by Julius v. Schnorr—all go back to a vision of Daniel (vii. 9), who beholds God as an "Ancient of Days, His

Fig. 69.—The fourth day of creation (after Julius von Schnorr).

raiment white like snow, and the hair of His head like pure wool." But the wearisome satire poured by the Old Testament prophets on the Babylonian idols—who have eyes and see not, ears and hear not, a nose and smell not, feet and move not—can be endured as easily by the Babylonians as by the Roman Catholic Church. For exactly as thinking Catholics generally regard the figures simply as representing Christ, Mary, and the Saints, so thinking Babylonians did the same: there was no hymn, no prayer that would be directed to the image as such—they are always addressed to the deity enthroned beyond all that is earthly.

Further, in estimating the "Ethical Monotheism" of Israel a certain moderation is desirable. First of all, the pre-Exilic period, during which Judah as well as Israel, kings as well as people, were the victims of a tendency towards the polytheism of heathen Canaan, as persistent as it was natural, must to a large extent be excepted. That being so, however, it appears to me a particularly unfortunate proceeding when certain over-zealous spirits represent the ethical level of Israel, even the Israel of the pre-Exilic period, as so vastly superior to that of the Babylonians. It is true the Babylonian-Assyrian method of waging war was cruel, sometimes even barbarous. But the conquest of Canaan by the Hebrew tribes was also accompanied by the shedding of streams of innocent blood; the capture of "the great and goodly cities not their own, of the houses full of all good things, of the wells, vineyards, olive-trees" (Deut. vi. 10 *sq.*), was preceded by the 'devoting' of hundreds of places both east and west of the Jordan, which means the ruthless massacre of all the inhabitants, even of the women, little children, and infants. As regards justice and righteousness in state and people, the ceaseless denunciations by the prophets of Israel and Judah of the oppression of the poor, of widows and orphans, in conjunction with such accounts as that of Naboth's vineyard (1 Kings xxi.), afford us a glimpse of grave corruption on the part of kings and people alike, while the continuance of Ḫammurabi's kingdom for well-nigh two thousand years might well serve to justify the application to it of the words: "Righteousness exalts a nation."

We still possess a tablet which, in most forcible language, warns the Babylonian King himself against any form of injustice. "If the King receives money from the inhabitants of Babylon, to augment his treasury, and then hears lawsuits by Babylonians, and permits himself to be partial in decision, then will Marduk, Lord of Heaven and earth, raise up his enemy against him, and will give his possessions and treasure to his foe." Further, in the chapter concerning love of neighbours, the place of compassion in dealing with neighbours, there is, as has once already been observed, no impassable gulf discoverable between Babylon and the Old Testament. One point illustrating this may be noted in passing. Over the Babylonian Flood-narrative, with its polytheistic features, Old Testament theologians make very merry, yet it contains one feature which makes it appeal to us with far greater force than the Biblical narrative. "The Storm-Flood"—so Xisuthros narrates—"came to an end. I looked out over the wide sea, shrieking aloud, because every human being had perished." As Eduard Suess, the renowned Austrian geologist, acknowledges, it is in such features as these that "the simple narrative of Xisuthros bears the stamp of convincing truth." Of any feeling of compassion on the part of Noah we read nothing. The Babylonian Noah was with his wife given a place among the gods—and such an idea would be inconceivable in the case of Israel.

Of the pilgrimage to Jerusalem for the Harvest-Festival, it is said in Deut. xvi. 11 (*cf.* xii. 18): "And thou shalt be joyful before Yahwè, thy God, thou and thy son and thy daughter, and thy man-servant and thy maid-servant"—what has become of the wife? The position of woman in Israel was admittedly an inferior one from childhood onwards. We know hardly a single girl's name from the Old Testament which testifies whole-heartedly to any such feeling of grateful joy to Yahwè for the child's birth as is the case in regard to boys: all such endearing designations of girls as 'Beloved,' 'Fragrant,' 'Dew-born,' 'Bee,' 'Gazelle,' 'Ewe' (Rachel), 'Myrtle' and 'Palm,' 'Coral' and 'Coronet,' are, in my opinion, quite insufficient to deceive us in regard to the matter. The woman is the property of her parents, and, later on, of her husband; she is a valuable element for purposes of work, on whom, in married life, a large part of the hardest business of the home is imposed—above all, she is, as in Islam, incompetent to take part in the practice of the cultus. In the case of the Babylonians all this was managed differently and better; we read, for example, of women in Ḫammurabi's time who were allowed to carry their stools into the Temple; we find the names of women as witnesses to legal documents, and more of the like. It is just in the domain of questions concerning women that it can clearly be seen how profoundly Babylonian culture had been influenced by the non-Semitic civilization of the Sumerians.

How differently attuned the temperament of men is! While Koldewey and others with him are ever marvelling anew that the excavations there fail to bring to light any obscene figures, a Roman Catholic Old Testament scholar[1] sees

Fig. 70.—Babylonian clay figures of the Goddess of Birth.

"numberless statuettes found in Babylon, which have no other object than to give expression to the coarsest, lowest sensuality." Poor Birth-goddess, poor goddess Ishtar! nevertheless, though only figured in clay thou

[1] See Note, p. 222.

mayest yet cheerfully make thy appearance in this circle (fig. 70), for I am sure thou wilt cause no offence—as sure as that we all not only take no offence, but rather immerse our-

Fig. 71.—Eve and her children Cain and Abel.

selves with perpetually renewed pleasure in contemplating the masterly marble statue of Eve with her children (fig. 71), which we know so well. And when an evangelical Old Testament scholar,[1] on the strength of a passage in a Babylonian poem, the meaning of which is still far from having been certainly determined, moved by similar moral indignation, cries out that "the lowest corners of hither Asia must be searched through to find analogies for it," I, for my part, though indeed unable to adduce equal local knowledge, may, however, venture to remind him of the grounds on which our school authorities have so stringently insisted upon selections from the Old Testament, and warn him, when he throws stones, to be careful that his own glass-house does not come tumbling down with a sudden crash.

But immeasurably more important than this skirmishing—which my opponents have provoked—about the relative moral standard of the two peoples, is, it seems to me, one final consideration which has not, in my opinion, received the attention it deserves in the preaching of the "ethical monotheism" of Israel, or of the "spirit of prophecy" as a "real revelation of the living God."

[1] See Note, p. 223.

Five times a day, and even oftener, does the pious Moslem pray Islam's *pater-noster*, the first *sura* of the Koran, which closes with the words: "Direct us (Allah) in the right way, in the way of those to whom Thou hast been gracious, who are not struck by (Thy) anger [as the Jews], and do not go astray [as the Christians]." The Moslem alone is the one to whom Allah has been gracious, he alone has been chosen by God to worship and honour the true God—all the rest of men and nations are *Kâfirûn*, unbelievers, whom God has not predestined to eternal salvation. Exactly thus and no otherwise, ranging itself in this respect with a sentiment deeply implanted in the Semitic character, does the Yahwism of Israel appear in the pre-Exilic as well as the post-Exilic period. Yahwè is the only true (or supreme) God, but at the same time He is the God of Israel alone, exclusively; Israel is His chosen people and his inheritance, all other peoples are *Goyim* or Heathen, given up by Yahwè himself to godlessness and idolatry.

That is a doctrine in any case utterly repugnant to our more purified ideas of God. It has been expressed, however, in the plainest words in a passage which at one blow annihilates the phantom of an 'original revelation'—the 19th verse of the 4th chapter of the Book of Deuteronomy: "Lest thou direct thine eyes heavenwards, and see the sun and the moon and the stars, the whole host of heaven, and worship and honour them, which Yahwè thy God has divided unto all peoples under the whole heaven; but you Yahwè has taken and brought forth out of Egypt to be unto Him a people of inheritance."

The star- and idol-worship of the peoples under the whole heaven has, according to this, been willed and ordained by Yahwè Himself. So much the more terrible, then, is Yahwè's command, given in Deut. vii. 2, to exterminate without mercy, on account of their godlessness, powerful nations which Israel should find in Canaan, as it is said in verse 16: "And thou shalt consume all the peoples, which Yahwè thy God gives to thee; thine eye shall not spare them." This national, particularistic monotheism, which naturally cannot assert itself in sections like the creation-narrative, but which elsewhere undeniably pervades the whole of the Old Testament, from Sinai onwards—I am Yahwè, thy God—up to the second Isaiah's "Comfort ye, comfort ye, my people," and to Zechariah's prophetic utterance (viii. 23): "Thus saith Yahwè Sabaoth: In those days it comes to pass that ten men out of all the tongues of the nations (*Goyim*) shall clutch hold of the skirt of a Jew, saying: 'Let us go with you, for we have heard God is with you!'"—this monotheism which, as even Paul for instance admits (Ephes. ii. 11 *sq.*), allowed all the other peoples of the earth through thousands of years to be "without hope" and "without God in the world"—it is difficult to regard this, I say, as 'revealed' by the holy and just God! And yet we are all from early youth so overpowered by this dogma of "aliens from the commonwealth of

Israel" (Eph. ii. 12), that we regard the history of the ancient world from an altogether distorted historical point of view, and even yet are content with the *rôle* of the 'spiritual Israel.' In so doing, we forget the mighty historical revolution which was accomplished in New Testament times, beginning with the preaching of John the Baptist and Jesus—that dramatic conflict between Judaism, Jewish and non-Jewish Christianity, which lasted until Peter was able to exclaim (Acts x. 34 *sq.*): "In truth I perceive that God is no respecter of persons, but whoever in any nation fears Him and practises righteousness, is acceptable to Him," thereby breaking down, once for all, the partition-wall between the Oriental-Israelitish and Christian philosophical views.

For my own part, I live in the faith that the old Hebrew Scriptures, even if they lose their character as writings 'revealed' or pervaded by a spirit of 'revelation,' will yet always retain their high importance, especially as a unique monument of a vast religious, historical process which reaches to our own time. Those exalted passages in the prophets and psalms, inspired by vivid trust in God, and longing after peace in God, will always find a ready echo in our hearts, in spite of the particularistic limitations of their strict letter and literal sense —although this has to a large extent been obliterated in our translations of the Bible. Such words as those of the prophet Micah (vi. 6–8): "Wherewith shall I come before Yahwè, to bow myself before God on high? Shall I come before Him with burnt-offerings, with calves of a year old? Has Yahwè pleasure in thousands of rams, in countless streams of oil? Shall I give my firstborn as expiation, the fruit of my body as atonement for my life? He hath showed thee, O man, what is good, and what Yahwè requires of thee: nothing but to do justly, to cultivate loving-kindness, and to walk humbly before thy God"—words so cogent for the moral practice of religion (they are also found in Babylonian literature)—are still to-day uttered from the soul of all religiously thinking people.

But, on the other hand, let us not cling blindly to outworn dogmas, which scientific knowledge has overthrown, even from an anxious fear lest our faith in God and true religiousness may suffer harm at its hands. We reflect that everything earthly is in a state of vital flow; to stand still is synonymous with death. We see the mighty throbbing power, with which the Reformation infused great nations of the earth, in all departments of human activity and human progress. But even the Reformation is only a stage on the road to the goal of Truth, which has been set before us by and in God. To attain that, we strive humbly, yet with all the means of free scientific investigation, joyfully confessing as the object of our devotion—seen from the high watch-tower with eagle glance, and proudly announced to all the world—the emancipation of religious development.

Notes

LECTURE II

The foregoing Lecture was delivered on the 12th of January 1903 in the Academy of Music at Berlin before the German Oriental Society, in the presence of His Majesty the Kaiser and King, and of Her Majesty the Kaiserin and Queen. That this second lecture on "Babel and the Bible" should also be given before the German Oriental Society I owed to it as well as to myself, on account of the varied expressions of dissent which the first Lecture called forth during my seventeen weeks' stay in Assyro-Babylonia.[1]

That the German Oriental Society has not the least concern with my personal religious

[1] I arrived at Mosul, 27th April; departed from Bassorah, 23rd August 1902.

views, although it should have been obvious, has been emphasized in the new edition of my first Lecture (p. 89), *and, as far as I am concerned, will secure even more decided expression.*

It is my most firm conviction that, if only a little judgment be used, it will no longer be possible for the opening up of these theological or religious-historical questions to be considered injurious or even insulting to Judaism, least of all to the modern Jewish faith. Dispassionate, strictly objective discussion of the origin of the institution of the Sabbath, of the position of woman in Israel as well as in Babylonia, and of other related questions, can only make our judgment keener, only serve to further the cause of truth. In this way that unanimity regarding the value of Old Testament monotheism, which for the time-being is far to seek in even the Jewish camp proper, will gradually but surely be attained. As opposed to the alleged universalism of the Old Testament belief in God—though it has been supposed to be proved in more than one 'open letter' by

Scriptural passages—other voices of Israelites, possessing a knowledge of the world as well as of the Bible, have made themselves heard, of such significant import as is expressed in the following words, extracted from a private letter of the 14th January 1903: "Your assertion that Jewish monotheism is of an exclusive character, in an egotistic and particularistic sense, is irrefutable; equally irrefutable, however, is it, in my opinion, that it is this absolutely particularistic monotheism alone that has made it possible for Judaism to maintain itself for thousands of years in the midst of persecutions and enmity of all kinds. Looked at from the Jewish standpoint, the national theism has brilliantly justified itself; to give it up means to give up Judaism; and even if there is much to be said in favour of this course, there is still a great deal to be said against it.' Regarding the divine character of the Torah, indeed, this must be excluded from scientific discussion, at least so long as complete ignorance of the results of Pentateuch-criticism is regarded on the Jewish side as 'exact science,' and (corresponding to this) so long as a discussion of "Babel and the Bible," founded on such ignorance, is disseminated far and wide through the magazines as 'scientific criticism.' The really abysmal obscurity, incompleteness, discord—to say nothing of more deplorable features—disclosed by the attitude taken up by evangelical orthodoxy towards the questions raised by "Babylon and the Bible," fills me, who myself am sprung from a strictly orthodox Lutheran house, with deep pain. From all sides and quarters I am assailed with the cry that I have said 'nothing essentially new'—whence, then, I ask, this excessive commotion?

And while from Aix-la-Chapelle deep lamentation and bitter accusation of Assyriology is heard because "in the lecture Old Testament traditions are, without further proof, arbitrarily represented as borrowed from Babylonian myths, such, for instance, as that of Nebuchadnezzar's madness," in the columns of a journal of middle Germany an 'orthodox pastor' exclaims, "I am fighting against a blind foe," because the historical books of the Bible, as a matter of fact, contained "neither the story of Balaam's ass, nor of the sun standing still, nor of the fall of the walls of Jericho, nor of the fish which swallows Jonah, nor of Nebuchadnezzar's madness—all of them accounts whose historical trustworthiness may well be contested even according to orthodox views." So that even evangelical orthodoxy sets aside 'revelations' which seem to it no longer in accord with the spirit of the age: will it not once for all condescend to an open confession, and explain without equivocation what books and narratives it thinks proper to strike out from 'Holy Scripture'?

One of the first and most meritorious of so-called positive investigators in the domain of the Old Testament, Professor Ernst Sellin of Vienna, in his "Notes on *Babel and the Bible*" (in the *Neue Freie Presse* of January 25, 1903) on the one hand cheerfully acknowledges the "absolutely incalculable amount of help, elucidation, and correction that Old Testament investigation owes to the decipherment of the Babylonian inscriptions, in the matter of grammar and lexicography, as well as in the history of culture and pure history," yet, on the other, he is of opinion that I, when I "argue against the fact of a divine revelation in the Bible on the strength of the Song of Songs and of growth of tradition out of material derived from heterogeneous sources, have appeared on the scene exactly a hundred years too late." Such a statement as this last can only be described as one of the grossest exaggerations that could possibly have been uttered. When my dear father, Franz Delitzsch, saw himself compelled, towards the end of his life, by the weight of the facts of Old Testament textual criticism, to make, in the case of Genesis, the smallest possible concessions, he was persecuted, even on his deathbed (1890), by the warnings of whole synods. The prodigious commotion, again, excited by my second Lecture serves to show convincingly enough that in quarters from which Church and school are governed an essentially different view from that of my highly-esteemed critic prevails.

Every individual clergyman, who has been a diligent student at the university, does, it is true, pay homage to freer views, but, all the same, school-teaching and religious instruction remain unaffected, and this is the almost intolerable discord against which page 5 of my first Lecture is directed. And this discord widens ever more profoundly. When, indeed, one of equally honourable theological antecedents writes (26th January 1903): "You inveigh against a conception of Revelation that no sensible Protestant any longer shares; it was that of the old Lutheran Dogmatists. . . . All divine revelation is, of course, subject to human mediation, and must therefore have been developed by a gradual process, historically," he describes exactly the standpoint that I myself advocate, only that I regard the conception of 'divine revelation' in the sense held by the Church and "of (a human) development by a gradual process historically" as the most opposed and absolutely irreconcilable ideas imaginable. Let it be one thing or the other! *I* believe that in the Old Testament we have to deal with a process of development effected or permitted by God like any other earthly product, but, for the rest, of a purely human and historical character, in which God has *not* intervened through 'special, supernatural revelation.' Old Testament monotheism plainly shows itself to be such a process marked by progress from the incomplete to the complete, from the false to the more true, here and there indeed by occasional retrogression, and it seems to me inconceivable to see at each single stage of this development a 'revelation' of the absolute, complete Truth, which is God. The attenuation of the original idea of revelation—so deeply rooted in ancient Oriental conceptions—which began with the abandonment of verbal inspiration on the part of the evangelical as well as of Catholic theology, and

Church even, and irretrievably divested the Old Testament of its character as the 'Word of God,' meant, it seems to me, the end of the theological and the beginning of the religious-historical treatment of the Old Testament. The Catholic Church, too, even if it does so more slowly, will not always be able to hold itself aloof from the results of modern science, as perhaps sundry slight indications already tend to show.

The resurrection of the Babylonian-Assyrian literature which, certainly not without God's will, is being accomplished in our time, and which has suddenly taken its place by the side of the only literature also of the hither-Asiatic world—the old Hebrew—that, up to that time, had survived from the past, is ever constraining us anew with irresistible force to undertake a revision of our conception of revelation which is bound up with the Old Testament. May the conviction make headway and grow, ever more and more, that only by a dispassionate revision of the positions involved can the end be reached, and that neither while the controversy rages, nor if and when it shall be brought nearer to its conclusion, can our heart-religion, our heart-fellowship with God, suffer harm or loss.

P. 153. The photographs of the letter from Chalach I owe to the kindness of the Director of the Assyrian-Babylonian Department of the British Museum, Dr E. Wallis Budge.

P. 166. The words above cited are derived from an essay by Walter Andrae, in which he describes in detail the painted representations in relief on brick of the wild ox as well as of the Dragon (Ṣirruš).

P. 169, l. 4. Eberhard Schrader's essay: *Die Sage vom Wahnsinn Nebukadnezzars* is to be found in the *Jahrbücher für protestantische Theologie*, vol. vii. pp. 618–629. Dan. iv. 19 runs: Then Daniel answered and said: My Lord, let the dream be to thy foes, and its interpretation to thine adversaries!

P. 171, l. 23. "*Deutsches Evangelisches Institut für Altertumswissenschaft des heiligen Landes.*" This has now been started under the principalship of Prof. G. H. Dalman.—Trans.

P. 172, l. 20. "Midnight Sun" was the name of the ship which carried the representatives of the governing bodies of the Evangelical Churches to Palestine.

P. 184, l. 21. *Cf.* Lecture I., p. 35.

P. 192, l. 22. *Cf.* Lecture I., p. 70.

P. 203, l. 5. Although Kaulen (col. 464) speaks of "numberless statuettes found in Babylon," etc., yet he can only mean by this those that have been found in Babylonia generally. Therefore I have ventured in Pl. 19 to reproduce three small clay figures, two of which were excavated in Tel Mohammed, not far from Bagdad, and published in Layard's *Nineveh and Babylon*, Table VII., H. I. ("Some rude images of the Assyrian Venus, of burnt clay, such as are found in the majority of ruins of this period"), while the third is taken from Léon Heuzey's *Catalogue des Antiquités Chaldéennes*, Paris, 1902, p. 349 (No. 213). As soon as good photographs of the exactly similar figures found by our Expedition are available, these shall appear in place of those now published.

P. 205, l. 1. Eduard König, *Bibel und Babel*, 6th ed. p. 57.

Conclusion.

As in the case of my first, so also in this my second Lecture on "Babel and Bible," I shall be content to deal only with scientific attacks, material to the subject in hand. I am afraid, however, that I shall have small occasion, if matters continue as hitherto, to concern myself, in the execution of this task, with evangelical orthodoxy. The method of conducting hostilities adopted by this section, especially by the Evangelical Orthodox Press, fills me with the deepest abhorrence. In the *Evangelische Kirchenzeitung*, founded by the revered Hengstenburg, one of its principal contributors, the Rev. P. Wolff, of Friedersdorf bei Seelow, writes (No. 4, January 25, 1903) as follows :—

"Following on the proofs which Delitzsch has already given, we must expect that in his next Lecture he will point out that how profoundly inferior the views of Christendom regarding marriage are to the Babylonian, is shewn by the flight of the Saxon Crown-Princess. No Babylonian princess eloped with the tutor of her children": and again, "Delitzsch intends to deliver a further lecture on Babylon and the New Testament; perhaps he will give us as a supplement to it something on the theme of 'Babel and Berlin': in that connection also many points of contact could be adduced. I might be able to offer a small contribution to it myself. It has been proved by the latest discoveries that the Prussian orders are derived from Babylon.

"On the monolith of Samsî-Rammân IV., preserved in the British Museum, this king wears, on a band round the neck, depending on the breast, a cross, which appears to be exactly like a modern decoration. How our comprehension of the real meaning of the orders is enlightened by this latest discovery! The order of the Red Eagle of the fourth class was already bestowed in Babylon! Thus as the origin of our orders is derived beyond all doubt from Babylon, so therefore it is proved that our modern culture is steeped through and through with that of Babylon." What a depth of spiritual and moral levity finds expression in these words of a German clergyman! And such samples could be multiplied tenfold!

As against this I welcome, as an Evangelical Christian, with feelings of deep gratitude and pleasure, the discussion of my Lecture by the Rev. Dr. Friedrich Jeremias of Dresden (in the *Dresdner Journal* of 4th February 1903), which, though disputing my conclusions (as was to be expected), is, both as to form and substance, a truly noble pronouncement.

The third (final) Lecture on "Babylon and the Bible" will be delivered as soon as opinion on the views expounded in my first and this second Lecture shall have become clear and settled. It will show that it lies much closer to my heart to maintain and to build than to overthrow and make away with pillars that have grown tottering.